Sketches.

"I can't explain to anyone how one can so get to love a bird as to kiss every egg in its nest and to pray for them. The many little loves and pathos and small tragedies (of birds and animals) I have felt deeply and always when quite alone out in the country. I often wonder if they are all lost and gone. They were and are so much to me, and nothing to anyone else. I might try my best to get anyone else to feel what I do over them, but I never could." EAW

Ted Wilson.

Published
By
REARDON PUBLISHING
56, Upper Norwood Street, Leckhampton,
Cheltenham, GL53 0DU
England
www.reardon.co.uk

March. 23. '98.
found all over the Gorse.
Crippetts.

Researched and Edited
by
D.M.Wilson and C.J.Wilson

Copyright © 2004

Text
by
D.M.Wilson

Pterostenus.

Layout and Design
by
N.Reardon

Lizard. April. '96. Ted.

ISBN 1-873877-70-6 Hardback Edition
ISBN 1-873877-71-4 Special Limited Edition

Bramble.

from the hedge at the bottom of Briar Brake. Crippetts.
Ted. Aug. 27. 1896.

Head of a Slow worm.
Crippetts Wood. May. 12. '98.

Printed
through
World Print Ltd
Hong Kong

EDWARD WILSON'S NATURE NOTEBOOKS

D.M.Wilson & C.J.Wilson

Bramble.
from the same bush as above. Ted. Aug.27.1896
Crippetts.

All of the Royalties from this book will be shared between Edward Wilson memorial projects.

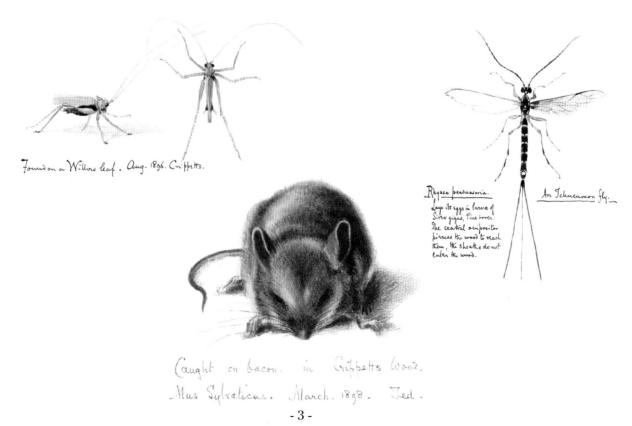

Found on a Willow leaf . Aug. 1896. Crippetts.

Rhyssa persuasoria.
Lays its eggs in larva of
Sirex gigas, Pine borer.
The central ovipositor
pierces the wood to reach
them, the sheaths do not
enter the wood.

An Ichneumon fly.

Caught on bacon in Crippetts Wood.
Mus Sylvaticus. March. 1898. Ted.

Green Woodpecker c.1908

Introduction

We both grew up with the Nature Notebooks. We are sometimes asked what this was like, to grow up with a house full of the pictures and relics of an English hero. However, to us they were always simply "Uncle Ted's" and we thought little more of it. We played 'hide and seek' in the irreplaceable Rum Barrel or Grog Tub from Captain Scott's *Discovery* (now a prized exhibit aboard the ship at Dundee) and were somewhat over-awed when the teachers from school visited to look at the Nature Notebooks. Indeed, visitors always liked to look at them, many of them prominent naturalists or artists in their own right. Their admiration for these volumes reinforced their 'specialness' in our minds and elevated them beyond the paintings by other friends or family members. Many of these visitors were surprised by the fact that Edward Wilson had produced such a large body of work outside the Antarctic. This surprise has increased in recent years, for our great uncle is chiefly remembered today, if he is remembered at all, as the heroic artist who died with Captain Scott.

From this perspective, it is probable that Edward Wilson's place in the history of art is as the last major painter of exploration art. This artistic movement was largely created by the fusion of scientific, cartographic and artistic techniques by the artist William Hodges, during Captain Cook's 2nd Expedition (1772-1775). The movement peaked during the nineteenth century but it is doubtful whether any of its practitioners realised that they were part of what is now an identifiable school of painting, least of all Edward Wilson who never believed himself to be more than an amateur dabbler. He admired and studied in great detail the work of William Turner, whom he considered the greatest of landscape painters. Turner, in his turn, had been an admirer of the work of Hodges. A clear link in exploration art therefore exists from Hodges, through Turner to Wilson, one based on aesthetic technique and vision, as well as geography. With the death of Edward Wilson, the major media for recording feats of exploration passed primarily to photograph and film and exploration art was re-submerged into the realm of the aesthetic.

Edward Wilson's effective successor was Peter Scott, emerging from his friendship with Captain Scott. Without this, Scott's dying words regarding his son, "…make the boy interested in Natural History if you can; it is better than games; they encourage it at some schools…" would never have been written and the history of conservation and of natural history painting would have been significantly different. Some books note that if Edward Wilson had survived the Pole journey, he would probably have become a notable British wildlife artist and illustrator. This has always been a source of some amusement to us Wilsons, as we know full well that he was precisely this. Edward Wilson's Antarctic art was only a small part of his artistic output. His repertoire as a scientific artist was prodigious. Nevertheless, whilst his non-Antarctic work might be remarkable to us, little of his British work has been published. His early death, just as he was reaching artistic maturity, ensured that he never achieved the fame of his contemporaries, Archibald Thorburn or J.G.Millais. Given this, we decided that we had an obligation to adjust the imbalance in the published material and so set out to publish Edward Wilson's Nature Notebooks.

Edward Wilson started drawing at a young age, his pictures being collected into scrapbooks from the age of five. It was in his teenage years, however, that he started to collect his natural history drawings into special volumes. These were generally arranged scientifically, not chronologically, with each of the carefully indexed volumes exploding with drawings, notes and paintings. He himself called them his "stock in trade". He fully intended to compile and publish them himself. He particularly hoped to produce something along the lines of the works of Ernest Thompson-Seton. However, it wasn't to be. He did use the notebooks as the basis of his illustrations for Barrett-Hamilton's *A History of British Mammals*, removing the mammal drawings into their own separate volume in order to undertake this work. He also started to use them for his work with W. Eagle Clarke illustrating *A History of British Birds*, until this project was cancelled. Nevertheless, the notebooks were in something of a mess when he headed South with Scott for the second time, never to return. So it fell to his wife, Oriana, to sort out his notebooks. Aunt Ory spent many hours arranging them with the help of Evelyn Ferrar, daughter of Hartley Ferrar, Geologist from the *Discovery* Expedition. Two large volumes in particular, were always "for Michael", her favourite nephew (and our father) and it is these that became known in our family as "the Nature Notebooks". However, there were numerous other notebooks, some of which were most certainly a part of the original magnum opus, that were widely distributed by Aunt Ory. The volume of British Mammals, for example, ended up in the Natural History Museum which later managed to additionally *Orkney Vole.   from life at Poynetts.   Sep. 14. 1905.*

purchase the finished mammal plates. The unfinished plates for the British Birds are at the Scott Polar Research Institute and many of the landscapes are in various institutions in Cheltenham.

As we set out on this project we therefore found, to our surprise, that the material we were selecting from had vastly increased in scope. We additionally felt that images such as the landscapes, which might not strictly be a part of Edward Wilson's historic natural history volumes, ought to be included, as they are an important part of his observations of the natural world. It was when we had completed the photographic work, however, that we received our largest surprise. With the images taken out of their context in the scrapbooks, it became possible to re-arrange them. Suddenly, instead of seeing pictures roughly ordered by Uncle Ted's scientific requirements, we were able to see the development of his work as an artist. This had never been seen or appreciated before by anyone because it had never been possible to re-arrange the images either within or between volumes. We found this so illuminating we decided to publish them in a chronological format. Therefore this selection from the Nature Notebooks is not being published using Edward Wilson's format but has become something of a biography in pictures, or a retrospective. This, of course, he would never have countenanced as he would have thought it vainglorious. What we have maintained, we hope, is the scrapbook feel of the original notebooks - with pictures leaping out from every corner in an almost bewildering array.

Once this chronological format had been decided upon, we entered on a rather fruitless search for his original Grouse Inquiry pictures and anatomical drawings. These are "missing", although they must be somewhere. We have found a few original images, reproduced here, but have had to largely reproduce from the published books in these sections and, since the quality of the period publications does not do justice to the subtlety of his work, the quality of the images on these pages are not as high as elsewhere in the present volume. However, we decided to include them, as they are an important part of his artistic and scientific development.

We have also gone to some lengths to digitally clean the pictures. Most of Edward Wilson's contemporaries agreed that one of his strengths as an artist was in his use of colour. We have done our best to reproduce the pictures in this book as closely as we can to the images as we believe that they would have looked when he painted and drew them a century ago. We feel sure that Uncle Ted would have wanted his pictures published looking as fresh as the day that he painted them - not with colours dulled by the acidification of the paper, foxing, tears and the other blemishes of time. However, for technical reasons, there are bound to be discrepancies for which we can but apologise. Additionally, it should be noted that due to our own technical limitations we have not attempted to reproduce these images to scale. This is something that he would surely have done and it is therefore a failing in our work.

Further, many of Edward Wilson's Nature Notebooks are covered in notes. He often annotated his own artworks, books, letters and diaries with observations and thoughts. In keeping with the flavour that this gives to many of his notebooks, we have reproduced a selection of quotations that give a reflection of his thinking and natural history observations at particular stages of his life. Additionally, there is a short biographical text at the start of each chapter, concentrating in particular on his artistic and scientific progress. This is not a full biography and if the reader is interested in such then we refer them to the three volumes of biography by George Seaver and the more recent volume by D.M.Wilson and D.B.Elder. All are listed in the bibliography, as are many of the books that reproduce his Antarctic works.

This volume is therefore unashamedly non-Antarctic. We wish to highlight the bulk of Edward Wilson's work, which is non-Antarctic, rather than his often reproduced Antarctic pictures. However, we have included a flavour of his Antarctic adventures, so that the reader will, for the first time, be able to relate his Antarctic work and his non-Antarctic work as a continuous development.

Nevertheless, ultimately this volume is peculiarly personal. It isn't particularly scientific, nor very 'arty' and it is unashamedly non-academic. For this we make no apology - we simply wanted to share the privilege that we grew up with and to make it possible for other people to enjoy a wider range of Uncle Ted's pictures.

We hope very much that you will enjoy sharing them with us.

D.M.Wilson and C.J.Wilson

November 2004

Acknowledgements

The pictures of Edward Adrian Wilson are now widely dispersed. To produce a representation of his Nature Notebooks therefore requires the co-operation of a large number of institutions and private individuals. We are genuinely grateful to all those who have enabled this book to occur, often at some inconvenience to themselves, through photographic work, archive access and through permissions to reproduce images.

In particular, we are grateful to those hard pressed individuals who keep access to our archives and libraries functional, often under considerable pressure. In this regard we are deeply indebted to the staff of the Scott Polar Research Institute in Cambridge (SPRI), which has a large holding of the works of Edward Wilson: in particular to the Archivist, Bob Headland, who has, as always, provided invaluable support; to Lucy Martin, the Picture Library Manager; and to the late William Mills, the Librarian and Keeper of Collections, without whose support it is doubtful if this volume would ever have appeared. We are deeply indebted to the staff of the Cheltenham Art Gallery and Museum (CAGM) for access to the considerable Edward Wilson holdings there and in particular to Steve Blake, the Keeper of Collections, for his enthusiastic support. Our thanks to the Bridgeman Art Library for the use of images from the Cheltenham collections. We have received considerable support from the Master and Cheltonian Society of Cheltenham College (CC) and our thanks go to them, in particular to Christine Leighton, the College Archivist, for her assistance. Our thanks go to the staff at the Natural History Museum in London (NHM) who have been unstinting with their assistance, in particular the Zoology Librarian, Ann Datta, and the Picture Library Manager, Gwyneth Campling. We are also grateful to Nallini Thevakarrunai, the Archivist at the St. George's Hospital Medical School (SGH), for her generous help. Thanks, too, to Gill Poulter, the Keeper of Collections at the Dundee Heritage Trust (DHT) and Sue Liptrot at the Cheltenham Public Library (CPL). We are grateful to all of these Institutions for permission to reproduce images from their collections for this volume and for allowing their staff to be so generous with their time in support of our project. We further acknowledge the publishers, John Murray, for their permission to quote material from the biographies of Edward Wilson by George Seaver.

We warmly thank our publisher, Nick Reardon, for the considerable effort that he has undertaken to make this project a reality.

Finally, we would like to thank the following for assistance with photographic work, for permissions to reproduce images, for their support, advice and/or endless patience: David Daly, David Elder, the late Evelyn Forbes (née Ferrar), Bill Fox, Maeve Kelly, Marie Kennedy, Harry King, Duncan Lawie, Don Manning, John Messenger, Liam O'Brien, Ann M. Wilson and Jean Wilson.

Needless to say, this book is our own, and responsibility for any errors and editorial choices rests with us.

Wild Cherry. The Crippetts. Apr. 12.'96.

Editor's Notes

In keeping with the historic period covered in this volume, all units of measurement are given in imperial values with the metric conversion following in brackets. It should further be noted that in the two sections referring to the Heroic Age of Antarctic exploration, the texts of the period generally use geographical (or nautical) miles. One geographical mile is equivalent to 1.15 statute miles or 1.85 kilometres.

Malvern Hills from the Crippetts, April 1896

1880

1880

1881

Common Brimstone.
Shurdnigton. Aug. 5. 1896.

PART I: 1872-1904

"All my religious beliefs are founded on the idea of evolution driven to its logical conclusion." EAW

Holly Blue. Henly-on-Thames. July. 23. 1896.

Aug. 10. 96.
Common Cabbage White.

June. 15. 00

Thecla cerri.

Göttingen.

The Childhood Years: 1872-1891

Edward Adrian Wilson was born on 23 July 1872 at Montpellier Terrace, Cheltenham. He was the second son and fifth child of Edward Thomas Wilson (1832-1918) and his wife, Mary Agnes, née Whishaw (1841-1930). In the family he was simply known at Ted.

On his mother's side, the Whishaw family constituted a long line of successful lawyers and businessmen stretching back to the 16th Century. In particular, they traded between Russia and the United Kingdom. Yet the family also appears to have fostered a certain amount of artistic talent having produced several artists over the years. A contemporary cousin of Ted's was the noted artist William Frederick Yeames R.A. (1835-1918).

Edward Wilson c.1876

On his father's side, the Wilson family were wealthy Quaker industrialists. Ted's great-grandfather, Edward Wilson of Liverpool and Philadelphia (1772-1843), left his children inherited fortunes; they wrote 'gentleman' as their occupation and in the early 19th Century fashion became dedicated collectors. Two, in particular, developed large collections of natural history books and specimens, Ted's grandfather, Edward Wilson of Hean Castle (1808-1888) and Thomas Bellerby Wilson of Philadelphia (1807-1865). Between them, these two brothers provided a significant part of the endowments that founded the Philadelphia Academy of Natural Sciences. Among the many books and specimens they presented to the Academy were 28,000 ornithological specimens, including Gould's collection of Australian birds and the Rivoli collection of the Princes of Massena. A series of bad investments meant that neither Ted's father, nor his brothers, inherited fortunes but were merely comfortable. It is said that Edward Wilson of Hean Castle called his sons into a room and sadly informed them that they would have to work for a living. Whilst his brothers travelled the world with the army and Church societies, Edward Thomas Wilson settled as a physician in Cheltenham. He had nevertheless inherited his father's passionate interest in the natural sciences. As a fellow of the Royal College of Physicians, he pioneered the development of isolation fever hospitals, district nurses and a clean drinking water supply for Cheltenham. He helped to found the Delancey hospital, the local Municipal Museum and the Cheltenham Camera Club. He was also President of the Cheltenham Natural Science Society, publishing numerous scientific papers. He also appears to have inherited, though not much to have pursued, a basic competence in water-colour painting from his mother, Frances Stokes (d.1891).

Ted's childhood was full of news from his Wilson and Whishaw relatives, from the far flung corners of Imperial Russia, the British Empire and beyond. Uncle Charlie (Major General Sir Charles Wilson 1836-1905) was a particularly good source of stories: he served with the Royal Engineers and was sent to relieve Gordon at Khartoum.

From the age of three his parents noted that Ted liked nothing better than to lie on the floor drawing. This resulted in his mother giving him drawing lessons. From the age of five onwards it is clear that the results were thought to be of interest, as they were collected into scrapbooks. These early childhood drawings are filled with an impish delight and imaginative flair, for his parents noted that at this age, he disliked copying anything from books. The vast majority of the early drawings, however, are either examples of his home-made Christmas cards or soldiers.

Whilst his parents were delighted with his drawings, there is no doubt that Ted possessed an artistic temperament to match his artistic talent. His moods were many and varied but always intense and often explosive. "The least thing" was said to make him cry, for which on one occasion he was dressed in his sister's clothes as punishment. These fits of earnestness were dosed with a mischievous sense of humour, just as his deep care for his family was laced with a strong sense of his own independence.

These moods also proved to be a challenge to his Governess, Miss Watson, from 1878, who found him "clever but boisterous" and so he was sent to a Preparatory School the following year. Although he was good at sports, even captaining the school 2nd XI, they never truly excited him, any more than his schoolwork. His reports were often full of the word "refuses" and he often had to forfeit his shorter school holidays as punishment, to catch up on his work. His father thought that he was "in his element" when fighting with boys from a rival school. At home the family often took long country walks and with his father as his guide, the Gloucestershire countryside became Ted's first love and inspiration. By the age of nine he had announced that he was going to become a naturalist and his mother noted that he would far rather have a naturalist's walk with his father than play the games of the playground. Ted started to develop his own natural history collections, collecting "everything he can lay his hands on". In particular, he and his father started to develop an impressive collection of birds eggs. From September 1879 these natural history enterprises became simpler when his mother took on a farm, *Sunnymede*, near Up Hatherley on the outskirts of Cheltenham. She was a notable breeder of poultry and the farm also produced quantities of fruit and vegetables for the ever expanding Wilson family, which eventually numbered ten children.

Much to his parents relief, his tantrums seemed to vanish when Ted hit double figures. Yet the intense emotions expressed in his childhood never really left him, he simply learned to hide them. The expression of his wild passions and keen sensitivity became increasingly sublimated into art. His first surviving landscapes, of Kidwelly in Wales, were drawn at the age of ten, in 1882, whilst among his last soldier pictures are those depicting the battle of Tel El Kebir (1882) where the British took Cairo from the Egyptians, and from where Uncle Charlie was sending letters home. After this date the focus of his interest begins to change to almost exclusively natural history subjects. His interest in blood and gore being channelled more effectively, perhaps, by "White the bird stuffer" who gave him his first lessons in taxidermy at the age of 11. He started to become more interested in his school work at this time, too. So much so, that he was sent as a boarder to another Preparatory School run by Erasmus Wilkinson, at Clifton in Bristol, as it was thought that he might be able to achieve entrance to a public school. The school set high academic and moral standards for its pupils and also tacitly encouraged the boys interests in natural history by turning a blind eye to a veritable menagerie in the schoolroom. Ted was in his element. In between lessons the boys went birds-nesting and Ted showed unusual sensitivity to natural history collecting for the period, never allowing all the eggs to be taken from a nest in 'mere robbery' but only taking one egg in four. His collections of beetles and other insects also became increasingly scientific, being correctly sorted and labelled.

Ted failed to get a Public School scholarship, so it was decided to send him as a day pupil to the Cheltenham Proprietary College for Boys. His academic work here was solid but never extraordinary. However, he excelled at games, at art and in the activities of the Natural History Society, being secretary of the ornithological section for some time. It was whilst at Cheltenham College that he received the only systematic art lessons of his life, as part of the school curriculum. His notebooks filled with classical drawings, still life studies and pictures copied from books to refine technique. At this time too, his natural history observer's notes started to become more complex and he started to gather his natural history drawings into separate volumes, with accompanying notes. This was undoubtedly influenced by the fact that at the same time that he started at Cheltenham College, his mother ended her lease on *Sunnymede*, taking on a larger farm near to Cheltenham, *The Crippetts*, near Shurdington. The fact that he was a day pupil allowed him to wander freely before and after school in its fields and hedgerows, making observations of the natural world, its wildlife and the changing seasons. He would often wrap himself in a cloak and leave the house before dawn to be in position in the woods before sunrise or take his supper up to *The Crippetts* to observe rabbits playing in the long summer evenings. Through his teenage years he taught himself to become a quite remarkable field naturalist. It is said that he not only learned to recognise the calls of the birds but could state exactly what the bird was doing when it made such a call.

Undoubtedly, his father had a huge influence on Ted's progress. He set out to teach his son the importance of observing from nature itself, to see what is present and to accurately record it, rather than seeing what is desired. During the summer holidays from 1886 to 1889 Ted carried out a remarkable set of botanical studies, under instruction from his father. The first of these were in pencil, but other series were in pen and ink and eventually he graduated to water-colour, though pencil remained his preferred medium at this time. By 1888 he was executing quite passable botanical, architectural and landscape drawings. His water-colours were still largely experimental, however, as his first surviving water-colours of more complex ornithological subjects, a Moorhen and a Hawfinch, dated 1890, clearly show.

It seems surprising, perhaps, given such an obvious talent and his enthusiasm for pursuing it, that a decision wasn't taken to foster it in some way. However, in the Oxford and Cambridge exams Ted obtained his certificate with honours in science. It was decided that he would enter Gonville and Caius College in Cambridge to pursue a career in medicine, like his father. Natural history and art were clearly seen as subjects for hobbies and not a career. In some ways Ted struggled with this belief for the rest of his life.

Edward Wilson c.1888

The Childhood Years: 1872-1891

Devilish lucky we brought the brandy, how should we have kept the cold out else?

A merry Xmas to you.

"Love one another in Truth and Purity, as children, impulsively and uncalculatingly..."
EAW

Tit Lark

The Childhood Years: 1872-1891

Views of Kidwelly,
S.Wales

The Childhood Years: 1872-1891

GREAT TIT

Ted.

BLUE TIT

Ted.

"There is such a rage for painting everything, chiefly birds: I set the example and now every fellow in the school has caught the rage..."
EAW

The Childhood Years: 1872-1891

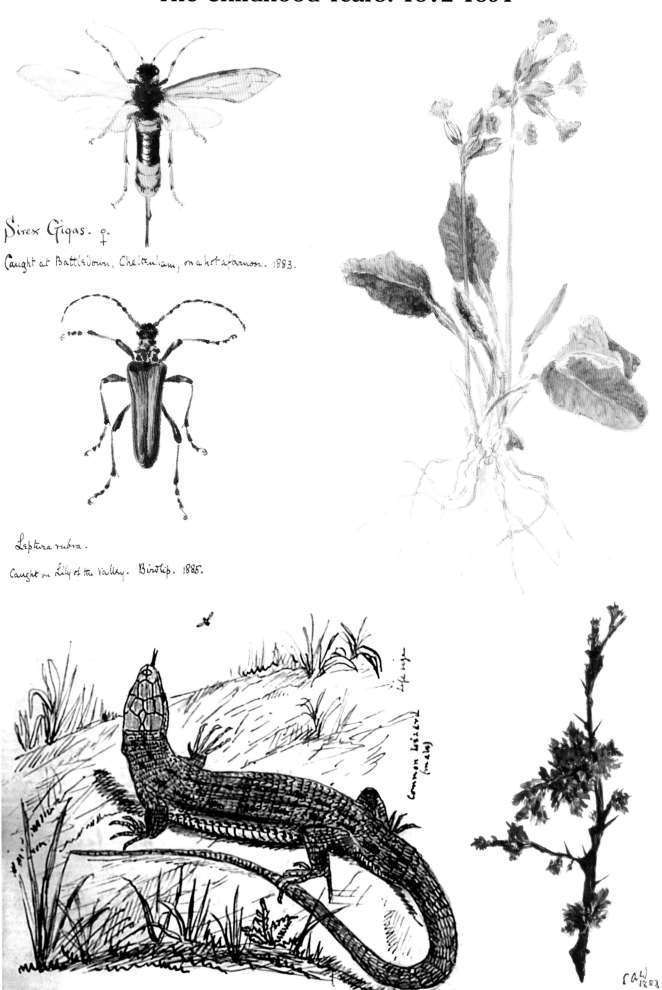

Sirex Gigas. ♀.

Caught at Battledown, Cheltenham, on a hot afternoon. 1883.

Leptura rubra.

Caught on Lily of the Valley. Birdlip. 1885.

Common Lizard (male)

Life size

Wood Sage *Teucrium Scorodonia*. Aug. 22. '86

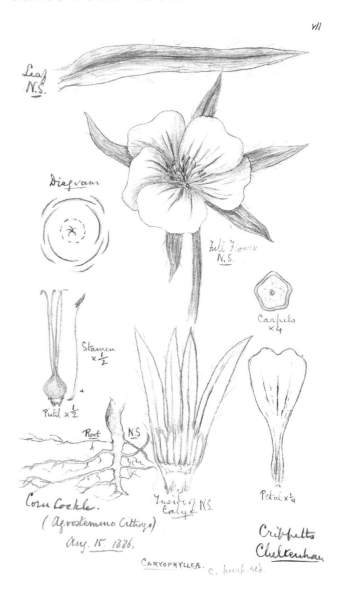

Corn Cockle.
(*Agrostemma Githago*)
Aug. 15. 1886.

Cribbpetts
Cheltenham

CARYOPHYLLEA.

"I blessed you for making me draw all those flowers and their parts, you can't think how they helped me in the Botany."
EAW

Deadly Nightshade
(*Atropa Belladonna*)
Aug. 22. 1886.   Crickley
SOLANACEAE   Cheltenham.

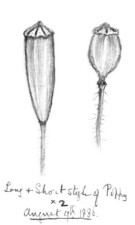

Long + Short style of Poppy
× 2
August 9th 1886.

Crippetts. 1889.

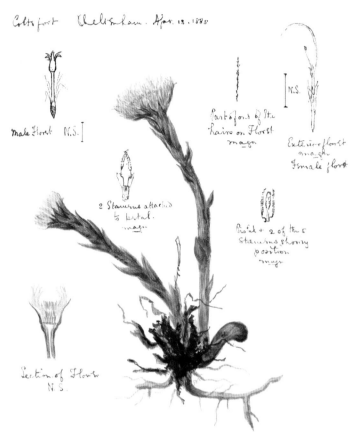

Coltsfoot   Cheltenham. Apr. 13. 1885

male Floret   N.S.

2 Stamens attached to petal. magn

Section of Flower N.S.

Part of one of the hairs on Floret magn

N.S.

Exterior floret on a Female floret

Pistil + 2 of the 5 Stamens showing position magn

Dicotyledon - Complete. Gamopetala - Composite - Coltsfoot (Tussilago farfara)

Violet. (scented)   Crippetts.   Apr. 16. 1888.

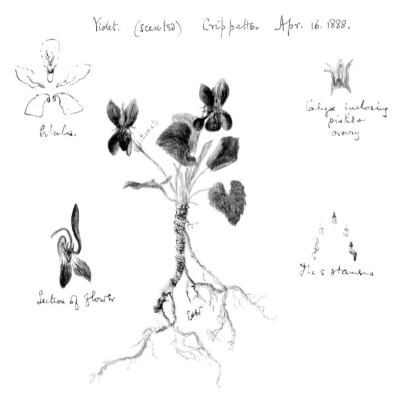

Petals.

Section of Flower

Calyx inclosing pistil & ovary

The 5 stamens

Crippetts. 1889.

Dicotyledon - Complete - Polypetalæ - Thalamiflora - Violaceæ - Viola odora

The Childhood Years: 1872-1891

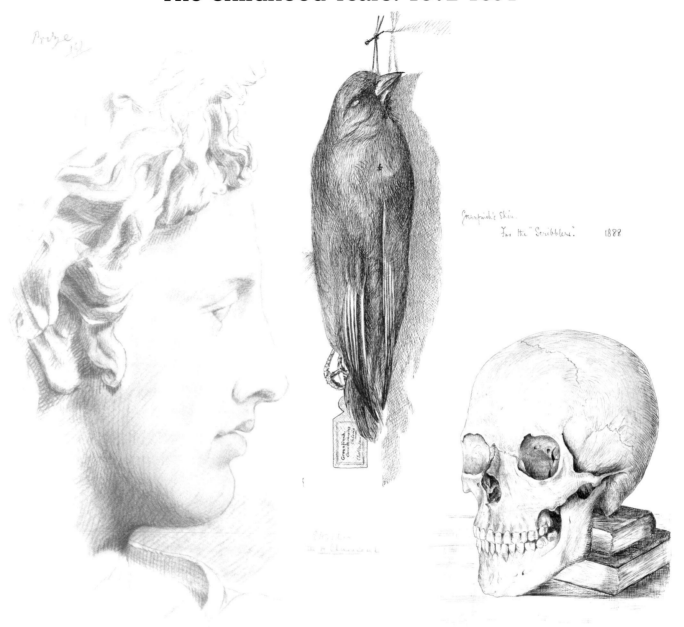

"What will you do with the badger if you catch him? Do try and leave some for me in the holidays, as I have been reading a lot about skinning animals, it is very like bird-skinning, and I daresay I might make something of a fox, badger or bunny."
EAW

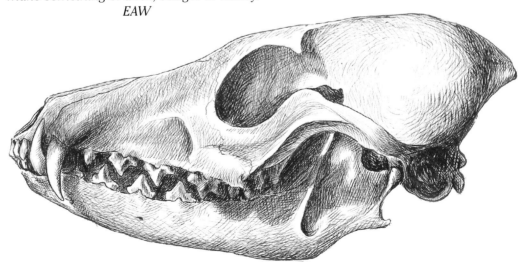

The Childhood Years: 1872-1891

Views of The Crippetts, 1888

The Childhood Years: 1872-1891

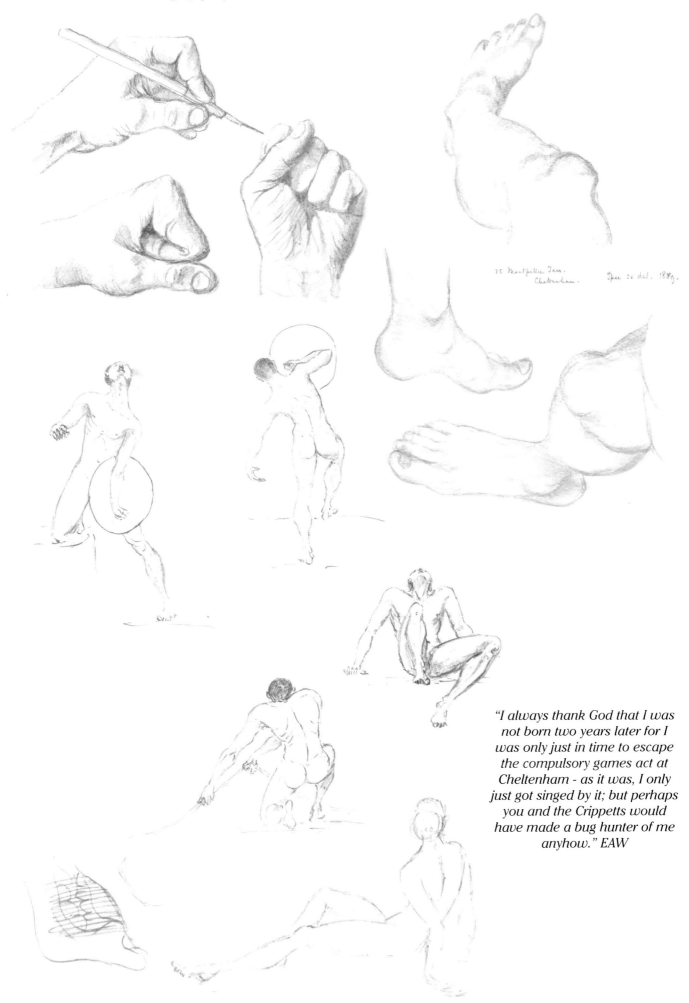

25 Montpellier Terr.
Cheltenham.

Ipse se del. 1889.

"I always thank God that I was not born two years later for I was only just in time to escape the compulsory games act at Cheltenham - as it was, I only just got singed by it; but perhaps you and the Crippetts would have made a bug hunter of me anyhow." EAW

The Childhood Years: 1872-1891

Top wheat field, Crippetts. July. 91.

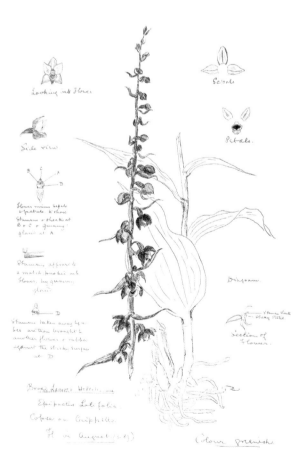

Malvern Hills fr. the Allotments. Crippetts. July. 90.

The Childhood Years: 1872-1891

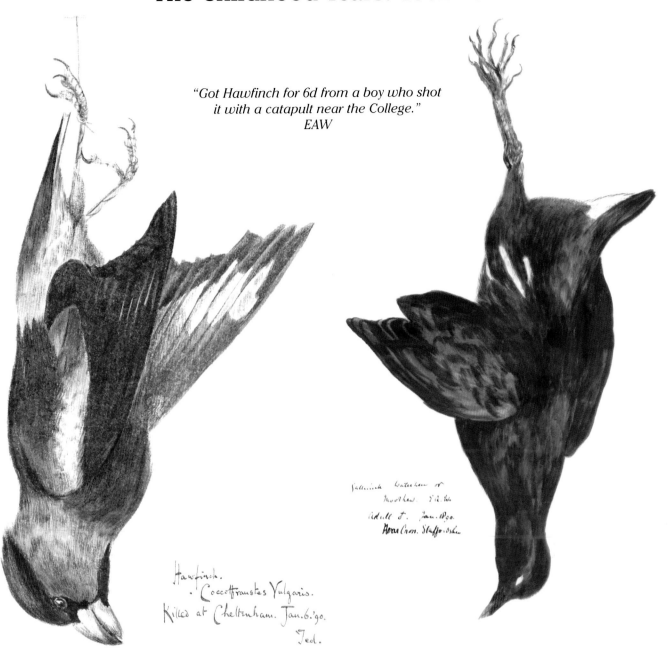

*"Got Hawfinch for 6d from a boy who shot
it with a catapult near the College."*
EAW

Hawfinch.
. Coccothraustes Vulgaris.
Killed at Cheltenham. Jan.6.'90.
Ted.

Common Grass Snake.
Crippetts. 1890.

Marsh Warbler. June. 1891.

The Student Years: Cambridge 1891-1895

The intake of freshmen to Gonville and Caius College in 1891 quickly developed a reputation for being turbulent. Ted was often in the thick of the action and yet somehow managed not to allow it to deprave him, preferring to draw witty caricatures instead. It was Ted's sense of humour which won him so many friends, as did his generosity with his knowledge and possessions. Ted also quickly developed a reputation amongst his tutors and peers as a mediator and peacemaker, a role which was to follow him for the rest of his life: his fellows trusted his moral judgement and his personal integrity. The rooms which he occupied from 1892, high up over the Gate of Virtue, became a centre of College life, the Master finding it necessary to comment upon the frequency with which his nickname, 'Ginger', was bellowed up at his windows. Despite such constant interruptions, Ted knuckled down to his studies, the several hours that he devoted to study every day soon paying off as he was awarded the status of an Exhibitioner, a small compensation for not obtaining a scholarship. Ted also rowed for his College, scoring several pewters. Rowing was a physical discipline that he particularly enjoyed, he felt that the treadmill of training was good for him and he enjoyed the thrill of the race.

Despite his popularity, in many ways Ted cut an isolated figure. Underneath the jovial veneer, he was still a sensitive and highly strung young man. He was critical of both himself and others. He disliked hypocrisy, injustice and self-pity, no doubt struggling with these traits within himself, and he possessed a caustic tongue that could be cruel. Ted constantly struggled to achieve mastery over himself and these faults, possessing enough humour, humility, self-depreciation and lack of confidence to avoid ever becoming pious. This deep introspection, typical, perhaps, of an undergraduate, appears to have led to a series of brooding self-portraits, something that he rarely indulged in, either before or after this time. It was during this time, too, that Ted began to formulate the deep moral code by which he lived his life. This was based upon a stringently ascetic reading of the New Testament. None but his intimate friends ever realised that it was this deeper spiritual level that gave Ted the moral power they so respected, as he rarely talked of such things, yet it gave him the inner strength and ascetic self-discipline upon which his future life would depend. Ted came to care little for originality and greatly for Truth, whether scientific, moral, artistic, spiritual or physical. Every aspect of life became, for him, a part of an indivisible Divine Truth with science, art and poetry simply different ways of explaining and experiencing a complex but Divine creation.

In between studying and rowing, Ted and some of his friends started "intellectual Sunday evenings", at which they would study and discuss art, music and poetry whilst smoking and drinking coffee. He particularly fell in love with Tennyson. Ted became active in the Caius Mission and in several College societies, occasionally reading papers on varied subjects. He also found time to continue with his natural history studies. He took the opportunity of long holidays to spend time at *The Crippetts* and to continue his long term observations of the countryside there. It is doubtful whether anywhere else ever quite filled the same place in his affections as the woods and hedgerows of the Cotswold countryside. When back at Cambridge, he continued his habit of long country walks, collecting and

Edward Wilson, with Milan, 1893

painting items of interest. His friends often enjoyed accompanying him and were astonished at the breadth of his knowledge of the natural world. On one occasion, for which he was much ribbed, he tried to jump a dyke and fell into it backwards, having to walk back into College positively dripping. His contemporaries commented that his rooms looked like a Museum they were so full of interesting skulls, bones, feathers, plants and other specimens. The walls and floors were littered with pencil and chalk drawings, which were his preferred media at this time. Nevertheless, he drew in pen and ink and was increasingly experimenting with watercolour. He amused visitors to his rooms by producing their portraits in water-colour, pencil or silhouette. On shorter vacations he would often go to London and spend time at the Zoo, the Natural History Museum or the National Gallery. It was here that he started to become better acquainted with the great art masters.

During the summer vacation of 1892 Ted and a friend matriculated at the University of Göttingen. His journey to and from Germany provided him with the opportunity to devour the art and architecture of Rotterdam, Antwerp, Brussels, Cologne and Cassel. He filled some 23 pages with notes, many on the great masters, particularly Rubens and Van Dyke and he commented, with surprise, that De Grayer and Sals were not better known. Whilst at Göttingen, he was astonished by the ritual duels of student life in the Landwehr Corps, such pastimes having long since been banned in England. In between his language studies, Ted most enjoyed exploring the countryside. On one of these many excursions he found a tree with a Red Kite's nest, to which he climbed and collected a chick. This became a lively pet, which he christened 'Milan', and it caused a certain amount of chaos back in Cheltenham. The kite eventually found its way to the London Zoo where it lived for many years. Upon his return to England, Ted found that his enthusiasm for the art collections at Windsor and the National Gallery were considerably enhanced by his travels; indeed he said that he had never enjoyed the National Gallery as much. His visit to Europe also inspired his interest in things around him in Cambridge. He cooked up a scheme with a friend to visit "all the sights of Cambridge" and spent a good deal of time studying and discussing local architecture and art. His developing enthusiasm for such things took him further afield to visit many of the great Cathedrals. A trip to visit his brother in Yorkshire and join a shooting party became a chance to visit the Cathedrals at Durham and York. This appetite for art also took him back to Europe with a reading party to Blankenberge in Belgium, which enabled him to make a return visit to Antwerp and to visit Bruges.

In 1894 Ted sat his exams, taking his degree with a first class pass in the Natural Science Tripos (part I). He was, quite naturally, utterly delighted and chose 5 volumes of Ruskin as a prize: his reading of Ruskin was becoming increasingly influential upon his own views on art. Ted was expecting to go straight on to St. George's Hospital to work towards becoming an F.R.C.S. and was astonished when the Master of Caius asked his parents if he might be permitted to stay on at Cambridge for another year because he was considered to be such a good influence on the College. Ted was not in favour and wrote to his father to say so: the work that he would need to put in to the extra exams (The Natural Science Tripos part II) did not, he said, sufficiently interest him. Neither was Ted convinced that staying up would help his medical career and so he generally preferred to get on with his 'real work' at the hospital. Nevertheless, he was persuaded to stay on at Cambridge for an extra year. Perhaps this was due in part to the sudden death of his youngest sister, Gwladys and Ted not wishing to add further to his parents concerns.

Ted continued to pursue his love for art and the natural world throughout his remaining time at Cambridge. He increasingly indulged his passion for walking in the fens, sketching the wildlife and making notes. His reading became pre-occupied with biographies of the great artists in addition to his medical books. A consequence of this was the life-changing realisation that even the greatest artists had had to study and learn their artistic technique. This realisation was liberating for Ted and began what his father suggested was a 'craze' for drawing and art. He started to work and to re-work his pictures, training himself in artistic techniques by seeing and criticising the work of others and accepting the critique of his family and friends. A new desire, however, was for art lessons that would train him to be a 'proper' artist and he harboured plans to take evening classes at an art school during his hospital training in London. As a result his notebooks, from 1895, begin to fill with images as he dedicated more time to natural history painting. In this respect his extra year at Cambridge was an unmitigated success. It was, however, an academic failure, as he failed his further exams. However, Ted doesn't seem to have been more than mildly irritated that he was put up for them in the first place. No doubt his extra year to indulge in art and poetry had been adequate compensation. He also carried off the University prize for diving. Many of the friendships he made with masters and fellow students during his Cambridge years lasted for the rest of his life.

Upon leaving Cambridge, Ted joined his family for their holiday at Nevin in Wales; many Wilson family holidays were spent in Wales and had been since his childhood. His father noted that Ted's sketching skills had significantly improved over the last year: his extra application in this regard was clearly paying off. The rest of the summer was, as usual, spent at *The Crippetts*, sketching, walking and shooting. Ted, however, was looking forward to getting on with his work at St. George's Hospital and to the possibility of art classes.

Edward Wilson at Caius College, 1894

The Student Years: Cambridge 1891-1895

In Caius Courts.

The Student Years: Cambridge 1891-1895

Dilton, on the Cam. Feb. 4. 92.

"I am working up a lunacy for pictures and poesie, in fact for everything of the kind..." EAW

Ely Cathedral. West Tower. May 1. 92.

King's Coll. Chapel fr. the Backs. Nov. 5. 92.

The Student Years: Cambridge 1891-1895

The Crippetts from Tombs's fields.

Leckhampton fr. Mustowe's fields. Ap. 3. 92.

Thrush. 1892.
Crippetts Wood.

The Student Years: Cambridge 1891-1895

"The old birds could be seen almost any day. Once one of them was followed by 2 crows, the kite settled on the ground and they left him. Through the glasses he looked rust coloured brown back all over, whitish underneath, whitish head, and broad part of wings and tips black..." EAW

Common Kite. Germany.

Wilhelmshöë. Cassell. June 27.92. Swans.

The Student Years: Cambridge 1891-1895

Ada and Longun studying in the Backs, 1893

Camb. Bot. gardens. 1893.

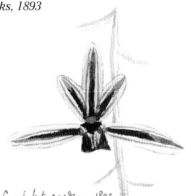

Camb. bot. gardens. 1893.

Cypripedium.   Bot. gardens. Cambridge 1893.

H. K. P. Young. Camb. 1893

Garden Warbler's Nest.
Grantchester. Cambridge
May. 20th 1895.

Cambridge. Barks·bte.

"Garden Warbler has eggs (fresh 4 eggs, May. 19. 95) Cambridge at Grantchester. The eggs were taken by someone, the nest opposite was left. Built into some young elm shoots a foot or two from the ground. I saw the bird well." EAW

Ted Wilson. 1895.

Sparrow Hawk. shot at Madingley· Cambridge.

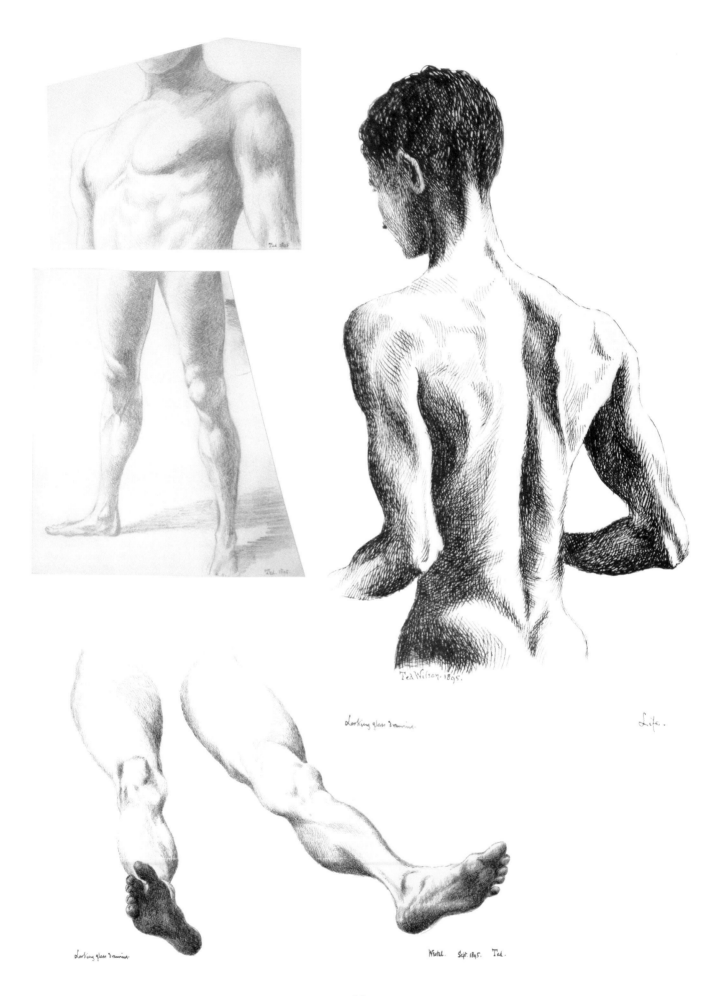

Looking glass drawing.   Life.

Looking glass drawing.   Natal.   Sept 1895.   Ted.

The Student Years: Cambridge 1891-1895

"I am no good at a gassing sort of letter, I don't mean that in a contemptuous sense but I never have written to anyone about my feelings, and I am afraid if they did get on to paper they wouldn't look too pretty. I've been told I am a 'dark horse' which is a modified form of hypocrite... I realised much earlier than most people what a blessing it was to have self confidence." EAW

Roach.   Caught at Cambridge.   Ted. 1895.

A rook coming to feed its young.
Cambridge, Trinity Hall rookeries,
Seen from Caius.   1895.

A cultivated Oleaceous shrub.

"Brer Mole"   Cambridge. 1895.
found dead. in rigor mortis. Grantchester.

Park Street. in a garden. Cambridge Apr. 23. 95.   (Yell.)
Forsythia

The Student Years: Cambridge 1891-1895

Perch, caught at Swavesey - Cambridge 1895.   Ted Wilson.

"The Common Shrew may be seen in April making its nest. You hear jerky little rushes among the dead leaves in some thick growth under a larch tree. Spot where it is and peer through some open spot you will see the shrew with a big dead oak or beech leaf in her mouth running back to her hole. Then there is silence for some minutes, then another shrill squeak and jerky rustling as she goes out again for another leaf..." EAW

French Partridge. found dead Cambridge . 1895.

Common Shrew.
Sorex vulgaris.

The Crippetts Wood. drawing.
Found dead on a path. Camb. painting.
1895.

Early Purple Orchis.
Orchis Masculata.
Madingley Woods. Cambridge.   May. 1895.

From Crippetts Window. Sep. 1895.

Spot.

Polly.

Canadian Turkey.   Ted. 1895.   Canadian Turkey.   Ted. 1895.
                                                                      The Crippetts.

The Student Years: Cambridge 1891-1895

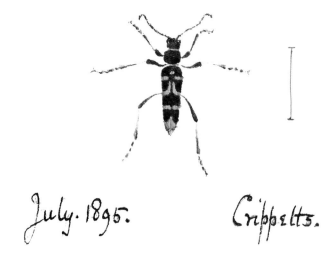

July. 1895.   *Crippetts.*

"In August and Sept. rabbits feed very late and very early. Sit out at dusk and as the darkness gets deeper, you can just make out what a number of rabbits are about. Sleeping out at midnight you hear stamping even in the small hours. At daybreak they may be feeding without a trace of suspicion quite close to one and stamp every now and again for no reason that one could see unless it is a call. It is done of course with the hind feet." EAW

Crippetts. Sep. 1895.

Crippetts Wood. Sep. 1895. (at dusk.)

The Student Years: London 1895-1898

Ted was rapidly at work with the second part of his M.B. degree. This involved long hours of hard work at St. George's Hospital and he was soon immersed in anatomy, physiology and surgery. Nevertheless, he found time to play football for the hospital and also to row. He took lodgings in Paddington and walked to and from St. George's which was at Hyde Park Corner, often taking detours through the London parks to hunt for "weeds and mushrooms" to draw and paint. Uncle Charlie rapidly introduced him to the appropriate people at the Zoo, so he soon had special permission to sketch in its grounds, where he spent all the time he could spare studying the birds and animals. Ted was becoming more confident in his abilities and potential as an artist, in large part due to his frequent visits to the art galleries around London. He was not always impressed with what was on show and was becoming increasingly convinced that he could do as well as, if not better than, some of the artists who had work up for sale. Yet for all of its stimulation, London felt claustrophobic to him. Whenever Ted could spare the time he wandered to the outer reaches of London, from Henley-on-Thames to Epping Forest or Stanmore Common, in search of a taste of peaceful countryside in which to walk and draw. For longer breaks, he still headed to *The Crippetts*. London, he wrote, particularly in the spring, left him feeling like a "soda-water bottle in an oven". Additionally, Ted must have felt family pressures intensely at this time, with one of his sisters marrying and another dying of Typhoid whilst nursing an epidemic in Leicester.

Ted's artistic abilities were soon noted at St. George's. His tutors and peers delighted in his predilection for drawing portraits of them during lectures and this soon lead to requests for the use of his talents. In particular, his skills came into demand for pathological drawing, his accurate illustration of diseased organs being utilised by the hospital museum and to illustrate papers by several of his tutors. Dr. Rolleston asked him to illustrate his book on the *Diseases of the Liver*, which he happily agreed to, although this wasn't finally published until 1905. Another colleague asked him to assist with some illustrations for his book on fishing flies.

One unexpected aspect to this was that he started being paid to execute pictures, sometimes as much as £1 for a drawing (about £70 in today's money). This in turn allowed him to retrieve his belongings from the pawn-brokers. It wasn't so much that he was unable to obtain money, his father would send him whatever he asked for, but he had started to experiment, quietly, with his strictly ascetic reading of the New Testament. For Ted, principles had to be lived, not to remain mere ideals. He strove to instantiate Christian principles in his life and this involved, in part, living a frugal existence. He prided himself on living on as little money as possible and when he had it, he often simply gave it away. As a result, his watch, or other jewellery, was often temporarily deposited with the pawn-broker. Perhaps this is why he never engaged in his desired evening classes at art school, or perhaps it was simply that he had too much to do. Already, his midwifery course required long hours in the slums and was depriving him of sleep.

St. George's Hospital First Boat, 1897
L-R: G.E.Orme; A.deW.Snowden; R.Abercrombie; H.H.Stiff; E.A.Wilson.

Ted spent what time he could in painting and drawing or in studying the works of the great artists in the London galleries. He admired the work of Japanese water-colourists but thought little of Tissot or the artists of the Paris Salon. Most importantly, however, he became "smitten to distraction" by Turner and spent many hours studying his pictures. Turner was to become an enormous influence on Ted's artistic technique, just as Ruskin had become a huge influence on the way that Ted thought about art. He increasingly sought to express these ideals in his pictures. Truth in painting, the ability to paint or draw whatever is seen as accurately as possible, became the benchmark of his success or failure. If he did not record something well enough, he tore up the result, no matter how aesthetically pleasing the picture might appear. So tightly was drawing or painting tied up with Truth for Ted, that its execution became for him a form of prayer. As such, his dedication to improving his artistic skills, which he worked upon with great tenacity, became a part of his asceticism. These deeper motivations and principles on which he based his life, however, were hidden from all but his closest friends. To his colleagues he was his usual jovial self.

His long hours of work and his experiments with asceticism soon started to take their toll. In October 1896, he was sent for a week's holiday to Cheltenham and *The Crippetts,* to recharge his batteries. Upon his return to London he moved his lodgings, taking up residence in the Caius Mission house in Battersea. Here he became engaged in youth clubs and Sunday school classes for the children of the Battersea slums. Occasionally, he took services, "talking, praying and singing in a positive reek of 250 Battersea children". The children suffered from fleas, lice and numerous medical afflictions. He continued to walk the 3 miles each way, through Battersea Park and along the Thames to the hospital, every day. He enjoyed the walk, it gave him a break from the hospital and slums and he could watch the wildlife along the banks of the Thames. If he managed to get away from the din of the traffic, he noted, he could almost believe, just for a moment, that he was in the countryside. By now, he was "dressing for Dent", whom he considered to be a first class surgeon, and was putting in long hours attending to accidents and emergencies, whilst preparing for exams. He became a member of the Guild of St. Barnabas in order to further explore the inter-relationship between his faith and his practice of medicine. Learning to love and truly care for some of his more demanding and self-pitying patients was proving something of a challenge to him. Ted was also starting to seriously consider the idea of becoming a missionary in Africa. He believed that his skills for mission work, doctoring and natural history sketching might usefully be given "free elbow room" in a life there, whereas he had his doubts about being in a position to combine all of his interests in a career in England. This thought was not well received by his parents and he was eventually persuaded to postpone taking any immediate action upon the matter.

Ted managed to take a short break to Brittany with his friend, Charles, exploring the area around Rouen but he generally preferred to go to *The Crippetts* for longer breaks. He turned down the opportunity to go to Paris as the captain of the hospital football team; he thought that the £5 could be better spent, although he was flattered to be asked. Given his love of art, this may seem surprising but perhaps the proposed trip would have left him no time for artistic study. For a short break from the life of the Mission he "got very fond" of the roof of the Mission house and would often sit up there to sketch the views over London. It was at the Mission house, one afternoon, that he first met Miss Oriana Souper. She was a friend of the Warden's wife. After tea, Ted excused himself to go and run his boys' classes and then retired to his rooms to work. Later, he stole down the stairs to quietly listen to Miss Souper sing. Their friendship was to develop slowly but surely; Ted at this stage in his life remaining a sworn bachelor.

Ted's appetite for art continued apace. He thoroughly appreciated Swan's chalk studies of animals, exhibited at the Zoo and the exhibitions of the Royal Institute of Painters in Water-colours. Here he admired work by Yeend King, Parsons and Richardson, among many others. He also went to see an exhibition of Millais' drawings but had trouble in fighting his way through a sea of ladies brightly coloured hats; a "Reckitt's blue dress and hat on one person will take the distance out of any picture" he dryly noted. However, it was his study of Turner's sketches that still most occupied his artistic life. Nevertheless, his method of self-teaching appears to have increasingly paid off, Ted becoming more proficient in the use of water-colour as a medium during his London years. Increasingly, water-colour drawing became his preferred media. He nevertheless continued to execute some very fine pencil studies.

When Ted returned to Cheltenham for the Christmas of 1897, his parents thought that he was looking frail and worn. On New Years Day, 1898, he started to read a biography of St. Francis of Assisi who rapidly became a role model for him. He was soon back at his hospital duties in London and also took on most of the work of the Mission, due to the illness of the warden. Given the intensity of his life in London, it seems little wonder that his health began to waver. By February of 1898 he was suffering a high fever, pains and giddiness, but he continued to work. After 3 weeks, he went and

Edward Wilson c.1898

consulted with Dr. Rolleston. After various tests, Dr. Rolleston confirmed that he had demonstrated the bacilli; Ted had contracted Pulmonary Tuberculosis. He was advised to seek treatment at Davos at once. It was a considerable shock both to Ted and to his family, Tuberculosis frequently being fatal.

The Student Years: London 1895-1898

Crippetts.
Barn & Cowsheds

From the Crippetts. Ted. April. 1896.

Pied Wagtail. Crippetts pond. April. 1896. Life.

" 'Butterflies and Bees' is a picture in this year's Academy and it just gives my idea of the six years medical training. The first three are the butterflies up here [in Cambridge], the three last are in Hospital in Town and now the sooner I get there the better." EAW

Ted. April. 22. '96.
Crippetts.

Shardington. Ted. April. 23. 1896.

Equisetum Magnum.

Cheltenham College Chapel

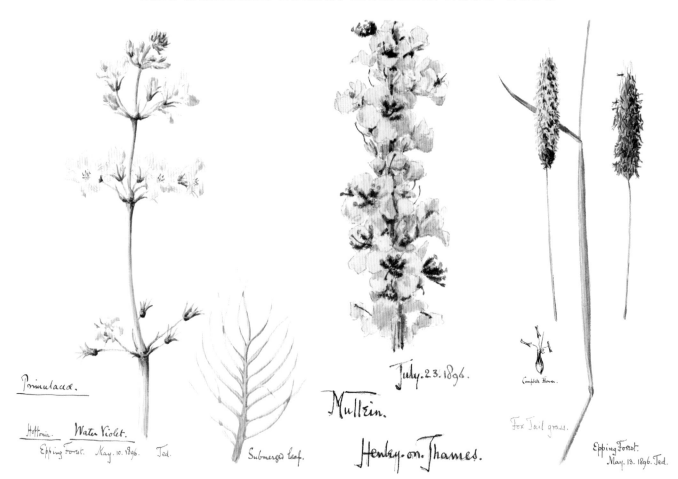

Primulaced.

Hottonia. Water Violet.

Epping Forest. May. 10. 1896. Ted.

Submerged leaf.

July. 23. 1896.

Mullein.

Henley - on - Thames.

Complete flower.

Fox Tail grass.

Epping Forest.
May. 13. 1896. Ted.

May. 1900. This bird is still well at the Zoo - in the Kite's Aviary.

Kite.

Four years old.

1896.

Kestrel ♂.
S · K · M

The Student Years: London 1895-1898

"Water Shrew seen in the stream down the Spain Grip. But is always getting caught in a water tank sunk in the ground in the kitchen garden, which dries up in Summer. Saw four of these running up the Spain Grip stream in single file. They were sometimes in the water, sometimes under water, and sometimes on the bank, but all going upstream as fast as they could get. Saw one feeding. Chiefly upside down, head under water, stern out. Every now and again retiring to the bank to eat what it found." EAW

Blackthorn.

Ted. Crippetts. Aug. 1896.

Sirex gigas, Crippetts. Aug. 27. 1896.

August.

These drop off during the winter.

Water Shrew.
Crossopus fodiens.   Crippetts. Aug. 1896.

Caught in a dry tank in the
Kitchen Garden.

Oak Spangles,
the gall of ♀ Spathegaster baccarum,
hatching eventually into ♂ Neuroterus lenticularis. Aug. 12. 1896.
Ted.

Drawn under a glass.

Brown rat.
Mus decumanus.   Ted Wilson. 1896.

Rat. found dead by the white gate. Crippetts. Aug. 1896.

Wasp's nest. Crippetts. Aug. 29.'96.

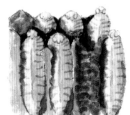

Cells with full fed gruks.
Cap with a hole contained a wasp just hatched

Cells with chrysalis and wasps
just hatched.
In one the cap is removed to
show the wasp's face.

One of the pillars, and
some chrysalis cells
with the caps.

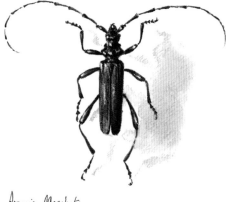

Aromia Moschata.

Musk Beetle. Tewkesbury.   Ted. 1896.

Aug. 1896.   Crippetts.

Ted.

Ted.
Aug. 1896.
Crippetts.

Honey suckle

The Student Years: London 1895-1898

Immature Cuckoo. Shot at Crippetts Wood. Aug. 1896.

"Went out after breakfast. Shot an immature cuckoo. Seeing it fly towards me it struck me like a Turtle-dove, and its head struck me like a missel-thrush, but it was too long in the body and the tail. Its flight struck me like a hawk's. But on taking flight I thought it couldn't be either of the three, so I shot it. Spent all day and the night in making a drawing and painting of it." EAW

Ted. Aug. 18.'96.
Crippetts.

Ted. Aug. 28.'96.

The Student Years: London 1895-1898

Vociferous Sea Eagle.
London Zoo.

Sep. 1896.

Starting his cry.

Position it assumes when alarmed.

Regents Park, on the path. Aug. 31.'96.

Hyde Park. Sep. 7.'96.

I
True length.

A small red ant.
Delamere Terrace. London. Sep. 7. 1896.

♀ Lesser Kestril. Tinnunculus Cenchris
Caught at Sea. off Scilly.

London Zoo: Sep. 1896.

Hyde Park. Sep. 7.'96.

The Student Years: London 1895-1898

Barn Owl.
London Zoo. Sep. '96 (quick drawing)

Peregrine Falcon.   London Zoo. Sep. '96

"Love comes to me by one channel only - the recognition of some beauty, whether mental, moral,
or physical; colour or form or sound; so long as it represents to me a type, however lowly, of my conception
of what is perfect - <u>there</u> is beauty." EAW

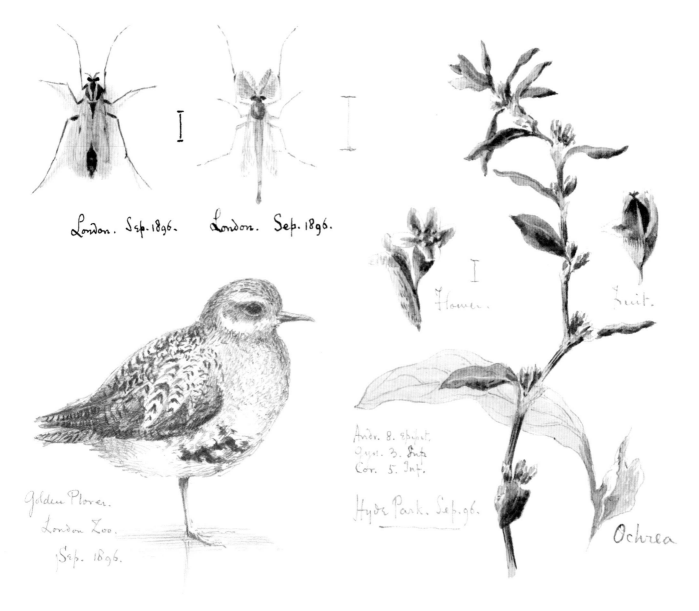

London. Sep. 1896.   London. Sep. 1896.

Golden Plover.
London Zoo.
Sep. 1896.

Flower.   Fruit.

Andr. 8. Epibot.
Gyat. 3. Inf.
Cor. 5. Inf.

Hyde Park. Sep. '96.

Ochrea

The Student Years: London 1895-1898

Gloucester Valley from The Crippetts

Cheltenham from The Crippetts

Leckhampton Hill from the Crippetts.

SURFACE OF LIVER WITH NODULAR HYPERPLASIA.

GROWTHS IN LIVER SECONDARY TO CARCINOMA OF THE RECTUM.

"If you see in my letters ... too much time given to drawing, Guild meetings, Mission business and things of that sort you must remember that all one's recreation in Town lies in such things."
EAW

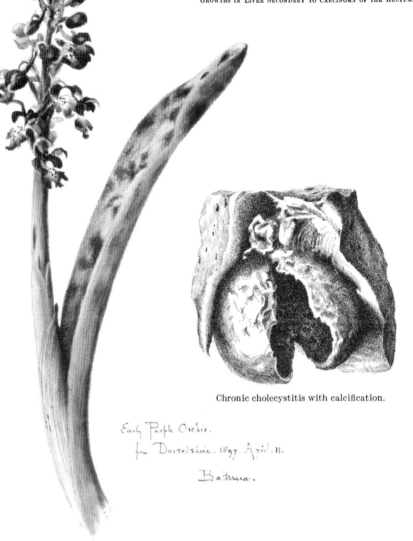

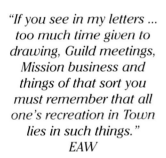

Chronic cholecystitis with calcification.

Early Purple Orchis.
from Dorsetshire. 1897. April. 11.
Bathnia.

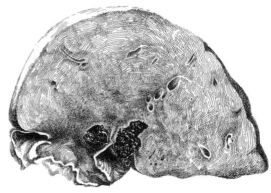

Papillomatous form of primary carcinoma of the gall-bladder.

Large intrahepatic calculi distending the right and left hepatic ducts.

Hyde Park. W.
Feb. 1896. T.

The Student Years: London 1895-1898

Knightsbridge

"London has a beauty of its own at sunset, which you don't see elsewhere. It's the smoke that does it. Crossing the river as I do now when the sun is going down is a new treat every day." EAW

Tawny or Brown Owl. Shot as it rose from under a holly hedge accidentally as a Rook! Crippetts. Dec. 1897.

Unfinished.

Partridge. Dec. 1897.

December.

Currant gall on oak. In the biggest of the three the grub figured above was taken.

Leaf of
Showing the larval burrow
of

Oak leaf showing the burrow of
with the central line of black excrement.

Leaves collected in December. 1897.
Crippetts wood.   Ted Wilson.

Crippetts. Dec. 1897.
On dead hazel, in woods.

Crippetts. Dec. 1897. Ted Wilson.
Peziza - Cupmoss.

The Student Years: London 1895-1898

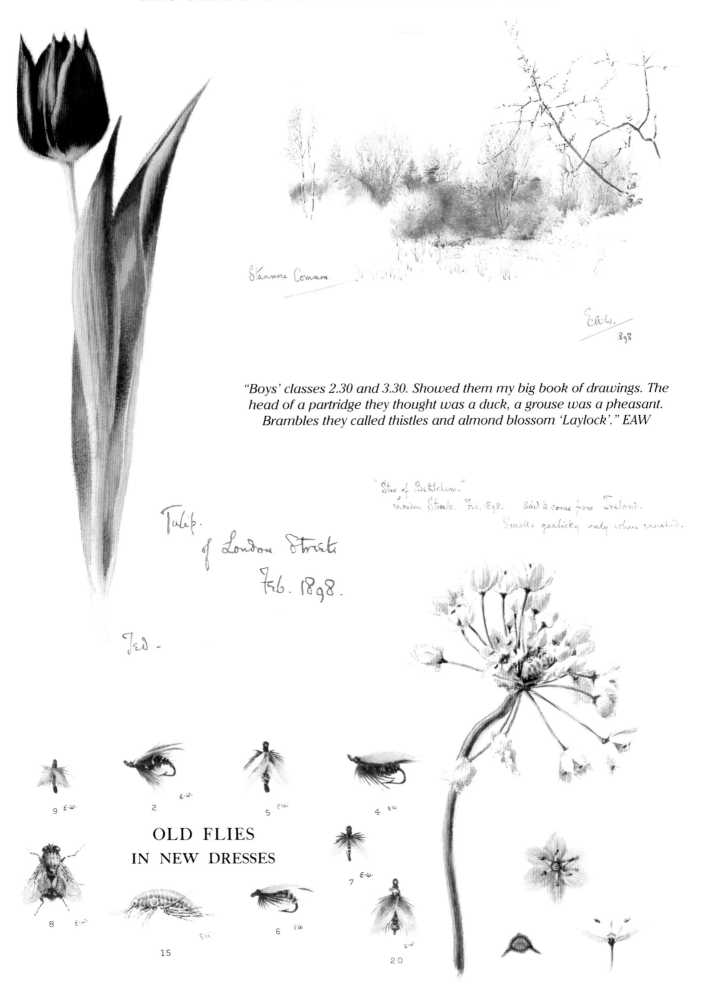

Stanmore Common.

EaW.
1898

"Boys' classes 2.30 and 3.30. Showed them my big book of drawings. The head of a partridge they thought was a duck, a grouse was a pheasant. Brambles they called thistles and almond blossom 'Laylock'." EAW

"Star of Bethlehem."
London Streets. Feb. 1898.   Said to come from Ireland.
Smells garlicky only when crushed.

Tulip.
of London Streets
Feb. 1898.

Ted -

OLD FLIES
IN NEW DRESSES

The Tuberculous Years: 1898-1901

Once the diagnosis of Tuberculosis was confirmed, Ted headed home to bed. He only rebelled once, when Miss Souper came to call. She had, quite by chance, taken a job as matron at a Cheltenham school and so called for tea. Even in bed, however, Ted continued painting. He had become interested in the blurring of colour boundaries in nature and produced the first in a series of colour studies. He was constantly delighted by the fact that the colours that could be seen were very often those that prejudice suggested were not 'supposed' to be there.

After a week in bed Ted felt better and was considered strong enough to go to *The Crippetts*. Ted spent his time in drawing and painting the countryside that was dearest to his heart, producing the most astonishing studies of Cotswold wildlife. Often he would sit in the woods at dawn, wrapped in his cloak, observing the natural world, with "*Modern Painters*, the New Testament and a good deal of pain" for company. He wrote that the thought that death was within "measurable distance" brought him "extraordinary peace of mind". The vibrancy of his painting suggests that Ted was far from morbid, however, and that he was starting to make real progress with his painting. He was often joined for short botanical walks by his sister, Pollie and by Miss Souper. No doubt they also kept an eye on his general welfare, Miss Souper acquiring the epithet of "the useful help". Since he couldn't wander as much as he liked, Ted collected an array of pets: newts from *The Crippetts* pond, a Grass Snake, and a young Red Squirrel which he named 'Puggie'. The latter was full of fleas and much to Ted's delight chewed up his sheets to make a nest. As the Cotswold Spring unfolded before him in all its glory, Ted was supremely happy pottering with his paints.

Edward Wilson with 'Puggie', 1898

Ted's *Crippetts* idyll was interrupted by an invitation, through some family friends, to go and stay in Norway for the summer. The main thrust of tuberculosis treatment at this time involved plenty of rest and cool, dry air. Dr. Rolleston thought that the air of northern Norway was as likely to be as good as the air of Switzerland and so Ted's trip to the sanatorium at Davos was postponed. He was soon in Norway, just south of the Arctic circle, staying near to modern day Brønnøysund. Here Ted found a new kind of freedom, with no social expectations tying him to meals nor anyone waiting on him hand and foot. He could do more or less as he pleased and so delighted in tramping the vast areas of moorland and forest collecting specimens and sketching. Nevertheless, the country was so vast that he often gave up walking and simply collected and drew the plants and flowers. Quite apart from his deteriorated health, which often kept him awake coughing all night, he found the clouds of mosquitoes and horse-flies something of a challenge. Nevertheless, the ascetic self-control which he had achieved by this time may be seen in the fact that he was able to sit and sketch mosquitoes as they bit him, a feat that few naturalists have achieved. Often he would sit in a cloud of biting insects, wrapped in clothing and surrounded by tobacco smoke, his hands and legs swollen with bites, sketching the shifting colours of the long summer twilight.

Ted returned to Cheltenham in August and was soon at *The Crippetts* once again, walking and sketching with his sister and Miss Souper. He particularly enjoyed walking to Gloucester to sketch the Cathedral as he admired its Romanesque elegance. Nevertheless, his tuberculosis was not clear and so in October, Ted was dispatched to the sanatorium at Davos in Switzerland, as had originally been planned.

The Sanatorium was something of a shock to Ted. His doctors insisted that he should do nothing. He tried to view his enforced idleness as a penance but he kicked against it at every opportunity. Perhaps as a result, he found the first snow somewhat depressing but soon came around to the challenge of trying to sketch the Alpine scenery and the complex colours of snow. His morale was further boosted through his correspondence with Miss Souper. Ted would sit in his fireless room, with the ink freezing in the bottle, to read her letters and write his replies. He lost so much weight and became so frail that the doctors finally agreed to let him take some exercise. Ted took full advantage, walking high into the Alps whenever he could get away with it. He also enjoyed skating on the lake. Nevertheless, Ted had to endure periods of inactivity during which he read and meditated upon the life of St. Francis or sketched. It was during this time at Davos that Ted consolidated the principles of ascetic mysticism by which he lived his life. It was here too, that he fully developed a colour memorisation technique that he had first conceived at Cambridge and which now came to fruition. It meant that he was able to make pencil sketches with colour notes and accurately paint up the picture later. It took quite a bit of practice and to begin with he often got things wrong but the one thing that Ted now had time for was to practice his artistic techniques. As Spring came to the Alps and the birds and animals returned to the mountains, Ted's strength began to return. He was allowed to wander far and wide and sketched almost continuously. He carried out series of colour studies that were critical to his artistic development, as he continued both to perfect his colour notation technique and his experimentation with colour. His progress meant that he was better able to capture the fleeting moment of brilliance in an alpine sunset. It was with some relief however, that in May he left the medical regime of Davos and headed home.

Ted's brief Spring visit to *The Crippetts* was again interrupted by an invitation to visit Norway. Still not fully recovered from the tuberculosis, he was rapidly on his way northward again and was soon sketching the vibrant colours of the Arctic twilight, in another series of colour studies. He picked up Sparrowhawk and Eagle Owl chicks as pets, along with a fox cub. These he drew in a series of pencil sketches that were later greatly admired by Thorburn and Lodge. However, the fox cub escaped and the Sparrowhawks were eaten by the Eagle Owls, so in all it was a somewhat eventful summer. It was crowned by Ted cutting his leg whilst out in the woods sketching. The cut became infected and so he was forced to return to Cheltenham, taking with him a pet buzzard. Once again he repaired to *The Crippetts* where the buzzard caused general chaos. It eventually found its way to join the kite in the London Zoo.

In early October Ted returned to London to take up his interrupted medical studies. Once again he took rooms in Paddington but his cough returned with a vengeance and he returned to Cheltenham. It did concentrate his mind on one aspect of his life, however, and he and Miss Souper were soon engaged to be married. Both Ted and Ory were delighted with this somewhat unexpected turn of events.

Ted returned to his medical studies once more, this time taking lodgings at Stanmore in order to avoid the pollution of London. He now had two months before he had to re-sit the second part of his M.B. exam and eighteen months work to catch up on. It is of considerable credit that he managed to pass. He then worked on writing up his thesis, *Yellow Atrophy of the Liver*. It was whilst at Stanmore that Ted took a long hard look at his natural history drawings and decided that anyone could paint or draw a dead bird in a classic Victorian-style plumage study. What he really wanted to do was to be able to capture the essence of the live bird on paper. He therefore set out to re-teach himself to paint and draw. At the same time he started to execute illustrations for *The Lancet* and *Land and Water*, although Ted had come to dislike selling his paintings preferring to give them away. Ted also returned to drawing at the Zoo. Here he came to the attention of the Secretary of the Zoological Society, Dr. P.L.Sclater who invited Ted to a meeting of the British Ornithological Union. He was subsequently elected as a member. It was at meetings of the Union that he met Thorburn and Lodge, who admired and criticised his work and he theirs. Ted also met with the bird artist Mr. Hammond, who was something of a recluse but Ted thought his work to be inspiring and considerably superior to that of Thorburn. Despite discouragement from his father and from Lodge, Ted was considering the idea of giving up doctoring and becoming a professional artist. He still craved proper art lessons, or even to see a 'real' artist at work. Nevertheless, his 'profession' won out over his 'hobbies', once again and he acquired a post as a locum at the Cheltenham General Hospital. It didn't last long.

In June 1900 Ted received the most astonishing letter from Dr. Sclater, informing him that the post of Junior Surgeon and Vertebrate Zoologist was available for the forthcoming British National Antarctic Expedition and that he would be a suitable applicant. Ted was utterly astonished. He was eventually persuaded to apply and successfully passed his interviews. He was taken on against medical advice and at his own risk but nowhere else had they managed to find the unique combination of skills which Ted represented. Three weeks before the Expedition sailed, Ted and Ory were married. Their honeymoon was dominated by Antarctic preparations but they were blissfully happy.

Edward and Oriana Wilson on their wedding day, 16 July 1901

The Tuberculous Years: 1898-1901

In this instance :—

α. The change runs the whole length of the colours from bud to fading flower, and they can all be found at one time in one head.

β. The change is from the centre to the periphery of each petal, in the natural order of colours, from central green to peripheral blue. but with a peculiar difference in the concentration. The green centre spreads fully concentrated as far as **x**. The yellow goes an eighth of an inch farther, fully concentrated and then **stops** and though it continues to get deeper and replace the green, it doesn't go beyond **x**. The red starts at the centre but goes farther than the yellow, producing a pink with the white and an orange with the yellow. Then the blue, if the starts from the centre doesn't affect the orange but makes on manve of the pink and a real blue centrally to the purple.

Why?

March. 1898.
Westal.

1. The unopened bud whose petals have pale green tips, in opening, discloses a pure white flower, with dead white petals, yet even here, the central is pink as compared with the peripheral greenish part of the white, yet you would call both pure white. The central eye is dull green, but its periphery more yellow.

2. Yellowish green - yellow - pale pink shading into pure white. There is now no trace of green in periphery of corolla.

3. Yellowish green - yellow - orange tinge - pale mauve - pink and so into pure white, but the white periphery is narrower.

4. Hardly a trace of green in centre - yellow - orange - pale mauve. getting paler towards periphery. practically no white.

5. No trace of green in the centre — pure yellow, orange with rather more red than in the last. The mauve has now lost its pink tinge in the centre and taken on a blue tint, while the pink tinge remains at the periphery. No white remains. This flower was completely faded and dropping off.

The Tuberculous Years: 1898-1901

Snow on Bredon Hill from The Crippetts

"... Things of beauty give me the most intense pleasure, which lasts a long time and can be recalled at will for days, months, sometimes years. There is something in it we don't in the least understand." EAW

Gloucester from The Crippetts

The Tuberculous Years: 1898-1901

Kestrel.

Wood Sorrel.
Oxalis.

Crippetts. April. 1898.

Spec. A.
Ted Wilson.

Stoat. adult ♀. Crippetts. May '98.

"Puggie."

Young Squirrel
(taken from the nest
April 4.98.)
drawn three weeks later.
Crippetts.
life.

Sparrows.

Crippetts. May. 1898.

The Tuberculous Years: 1898-1901

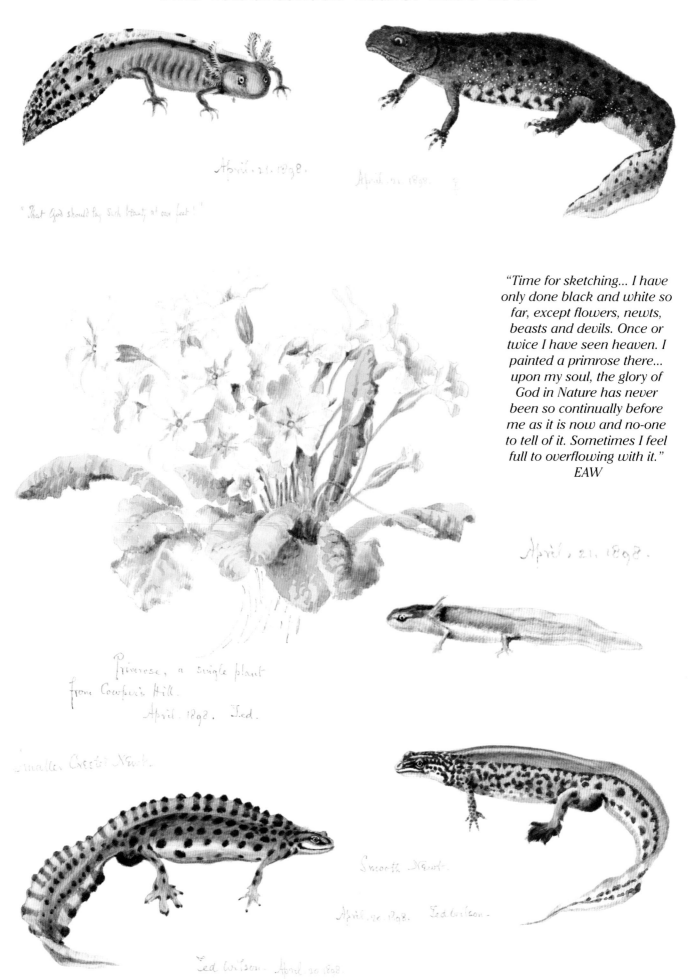

"That God should lay such beauty at our feet!"

April. 21. 1898.

April. 21. 1898.

"Time for sketching... I have only done black and white so far, except flowers, newts, beasts and devils. Once or twice I have seen heaven. I painted a primrose there... upon my soul, the glory of God in Nature has never been so continually before me as it is now and no-one to tell of it. Sometimes I feel full to overflowing with it."
EAW

April. 21. 1898.

Primrose, a single plant from Cowper's Hill.
April. 1898. Ted.

Smaller Crested Newt.

Smooth Newt.

April 20 1898. Ted Wilson.

Ted Wilson. April 20 1898.

The Tuberculous Years: 1898-1901

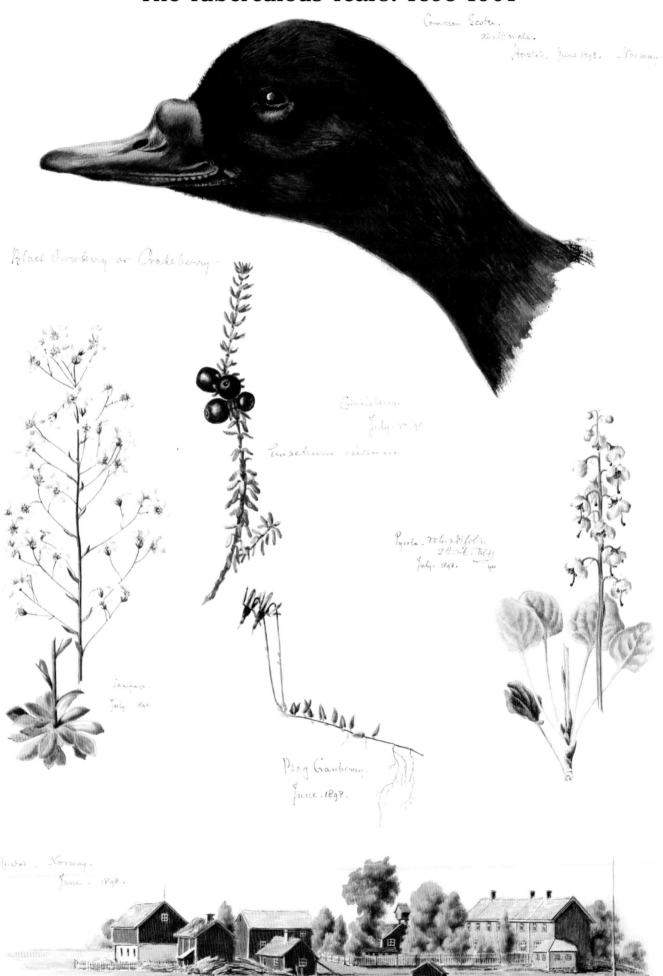

Common Scoter.
adult male.
Horstad, June 1898. — Norway.

Black Crowberry or Crakeberry.

Crakeberry
July 1st 98
Empetrum nigrum

Pyrola. rotundifolia
Stink Nells
July. 1898.

Saxifrage.
July 98

Bog Cranberry.
June. 1898.

Horstad. Norway.
June. 1898.

Grows in clumps on rocky mountains. July. 11. 98.

Cassiope hypnoidis

Norway.

June - July. 1898.

Dryas octopetala

A Cleg beast.

Bear-berry.
July. 20. '98. Precipice.

White Avens.

on Mountain tops. Snow level. June. 1898. Louisetta.

Arctostaphylos alpina

The Cleg Beast.

& his head.

Horstad. July. 1898.

Hungry.

Not Hungry.

"One has to take one's chance what with rain and clegs and mosquitoes and expeditions and no room of one's own to draw in; there are many difficulties… Clegs are big horseflies which leave a speck of blood upon the bite like a cairn on a mountain when it swells up. The bite is like a drawing-pin and itches like the devil. I use a clothes brush for the itching and then Hazeline."
EAW

The Mosquito Beast.

Horstad. July. 1898.

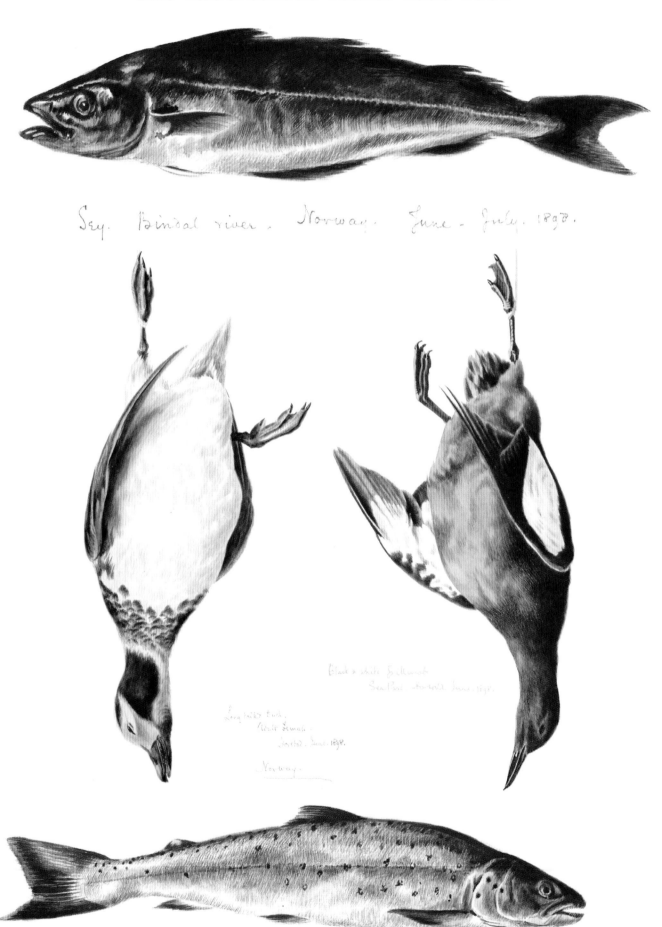

Sey. Bindal river. Norway. June - July. 1898.

Starved Sea Trout. Bindal river. June - 1898.

The Tuberculous Years: 1898-1901

"Very, very beautiful, with everything just draped in snow, the sun quickly clearing it off where it could reach it. There is something that suggests tenderness and love in the way in which these clouds, heavy grey rolling masses laughing up at the sun above, softly fold themselves right round a mountain peak. For a whole day long they will remain there with the mountain top buried in their embrace, and then at sunset the clouds will clear, the moon break through, and the mountain stands again above - but how changed, how much more white and clean, smiling up to heaven with a heart renewed..." EAW

The Tuberculous Years: 1898-1901

Sunset studies: Tingenhorn, High Alps, Switzerland

The Tuberculous Years: 1898-1901

Davos.
1899.

Siskin Hen   April 1899   Davos.

"I can't bear people who always take for granted that one's main object is to save up one's health and strength, eyesight and what not, for when one is sixty. How on earth can they tell whether one is going to reach thirty?
I think it's better to wear a thing while it's good and new, patching the odd corners as they wear out, instead of putting it away carefully year after year till at last the moths get in, and you find it's no good when
at last you think you will wear it."
EAW

Yerper. Hazel Grouse.

The Tuberculous Years: 1898-1901

The Tuberculous Years: 1898-1901

Norway.   Sunset. Ingelstad. July 1899.

Sunset, Horstad. July. 1899.

"After dinner we had one of the sunsets which gets all the mountains flaming in yellow and red and gold; one gets so many contrasting greys and purples in the shadowed mountains and the red trunks of the Scotch firs blaze out like rods of fire and the greens of the Spruces in the light all become orange and red… Then the snow patches become rosy and blue in the shadow and the sky tones up from a yellow into very light green and blue and then in a few minutes when you wonder what is coming next it all goes out and you are left with sober greys and greens and mosquitoes. It takes a lot of yellow paint and tobacco but the results are remarkable…" EAW

Rough Legged Buzzard.
young birds, about 5 weeks old.
Harstad, Norway. Aug. 1899.

Börridalen. Sylt. norway. 1899. G.dU.

The Tuberculous Years: 1898-1901

Lapp man with Ski.

Lapp woman on Ski.

"Sliding down the snow patches, in a valley we fell in with about 250 Reindeer, bulls, cows and calves. They have black mossy horns this time of year (June) and their grunting was very funny, you could hear them right up the valley. Many of them are belled. Their colour varies from a nearly pure white to cream or grey or brown. We met a Lapp man and woman, and I sketched..." EAW

The Tuberculous Years: 1898-1901

Willow Grouse. Winter Plumage. Norway. Jan. 1901.

Great Black Woodpecker.
Tropical gulley. July. 2. 99
Horstad.

Fieldfare Sitting
Horstad. Norway. June. 1899.

Young Eagle owls.
Horstad. Norway.
July. 1899.

The Tuberculous Years: 1898-1901

Jan. 1900.

Song Thrush.
Stanmore -

Great Tits

Blue Tits   Stanmore -

Jan. 1900 -

"Really I know nothing that I have ever tried to do which has such an absorbing interest for me as drawing. I feel that if I deliberately hid it away and forced myself to take to doctoring, I might be in the same position as the man who had one talent given him and decided he had better not use it. Not that I intend to throw up Medicine altogether. I should love to do some doctoring if it was only among poor people whom one might, if drawing keeps us, doctor for next to nothing."
EAW

Chaffinch... ♂
Jan. 1900 -
Stanmore.

Tawny owl sailing

Stanmore -   E. A. W.   Stanmore - from Loscombe Lodge Windows.
                    1899 -

The Tuberculous Years: 1898-1901

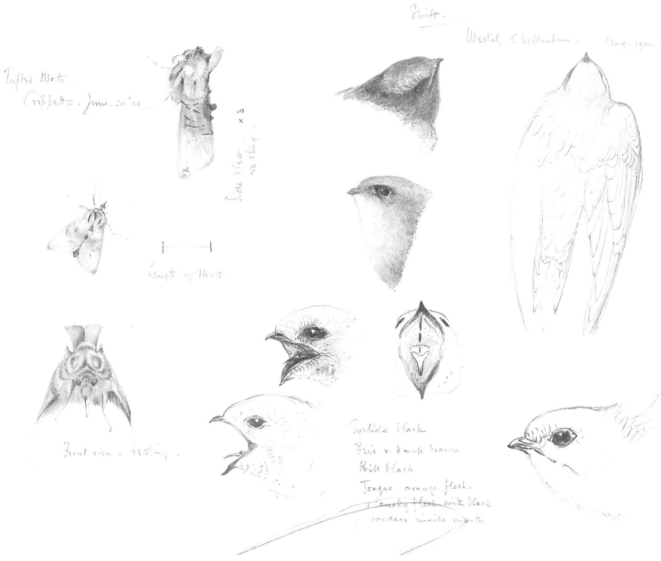

Swift.

Westal, Cheltenham. Aug. 1900.

Tufted Moth.
Cribbetts - June. 20.'00

Side view - resting. × 3

Length of Moth.

Front view - resting.

Eyelids black
Iris v. dark brown
Bill black
Tongue orange flesh.
Dusky flesh with black
borders inside mouth

The Cribbetts.
Leckhampton. 1900
Ted Wilson.

The Tuberculous Years: 1898-1901

Gloucester Cathedral

"The more quietly and privately one lives with God's own gifts, the more one fits one's self for helping others to see them. That's one thing I have always felt God meant me for - to show his glorious beauty to others who haven't had the opportunity of finding out the things that are so wonderfully beautiful in the most common country. My pictures are the realisation of little things that have been treasured up in my mind, little traits of character picked up crumb by crumb in fields and hedgerows, at last pieced together and put into the form of something living." EAW

Aurora Australis

'DISCOVERY' INTERLUDE:
THE BRITISH NATIONAL ANTARCTIC EXPEDITION
1901-1904

"Sketching in the Antarctic is not all joy, for apart from the fact that your fingers are all thumbs and you don't know what or where they are till they warm up again, you can only sketch when your eyes stop running - one eye at a time through a narrow slit in snow-goggles." EAW

The British National Antarctic Expedition: 1901-1904

The British National Antarctic Expedition was part of a co-ordinated pan-European campaign to unveil the frigid enigmas of Antarctica. Explorers had ventured South before but surprisingly little was known; it wasn't even clear whether a continent existed in the hole on the map. Ted was caught up in a whirl of preparations for heading into the unknown aboard the purpose built ship *Discovery*, under Commander Robert Falcon Scott. He brushed up his skills in taxidermy, on the identification of whales and dolphins and read up on subjects such as scurvy. He also designed the Expedition crest for use on crockery and note-paper. Much of Ted's time was spent in the Natural History Museum working on the specimens from the recently returned *Southern Cross* expedition

Weddell Seal plate, 'Southern Cross' expedition report, 1901

and he wrote the report on the seals. Ted's first paper on Antarctic fauna was therefore published before he had ever been South and the illustrations, whilst competent, clearly reflect this. They represent the very style of 'wooden' wildlife art from dead specimens that Ted so wanted to move away from. In this case, however, he had little choice. Upon return, his artwork for the seals in the *Discovery* expedition reports would be intimate portraits of live animals.

Discovery sailed from the Solent on 6 August 1901 after an inspection by the King and Queen. Ted watched Ory slowly disappear from view. As they sailed South, he soon found himself to be in his element, working with the other scientists to uncover the mysteries of the ocean. He commenced the large biological collections of the Expedition, collecting and painting seabirds. These became his first serious ornithological watercolours. In addition to painting the specimens which were destined for British Museums, Ted also enjoyed sitting and sketching birds from the ship in all weathers. He was later to become noted for his artistic achievement in successfully capturing the flight of seabirds on paper, in a period when most artists were still painting seabirds as stuffed specimens. Ted, the amateur dabbler, was by this time inadvertently working at the forefront of modern wildlife painting and seabird ornithology. This isn't to say that there weren't difficulties; he had to work out how to keep his paper dry and to produce an accurate sketch of a seabird whilst the ship was swinging through 30°.

There were challenges in other ways too. Ted found that it took him a considerable effort to adjust to the Navy way of doing things, despite his admiration for several of the officers, including Scott. His most withering criticism, as always, was reserved for those with large egos who didn't pull their weight. He still occasionally let slip a caustic remark and so became known as 'Bill the cynic' to some aboard. However, he viewed his confinement with such men as a part of his ascetic progress: it challenged him to maintain self-control. He gradually earned the respect of his shipmates both for the application of his numerous skills and his diplomacy. As at school and Cambridge, many of his shipmates turned to him as a trusted confidante.

Edward Wilson with 'Discovery' life ring, August 1901

Sailing via Madeira, South Trinidad, South Africa and Macquarie Island, *Discovery* finally sailed from New Zealand on 24 December and headed for the Ross Sea. Just after midnight on 8 January 1902 they sighted the coast of Victoria Land. From here Ted started on a series of panoramic sketches, producing a unique cartographic record of the coastline of Victoria Land from Cape Adare to Ross Island. He also produced numerous sketches of the Great Ice Barrier and the newly discovered King Edward VII Land.

Eventually securing their winter quarters at Ross Island, *Discovery* settled in for the winter. Ted was busy assisting with the wider scientific programmes as well as his own vertebrate zoology work and medical duties. He walked to the top of Crater Hill with Ernest Shackleton almost daily to read the temperatures at the outlying meteorological station. It was during such walks that he sketched, under extremely difficult conditions, some of the phenomena of an Antarctic winter. Able to work in pencil for only a few minutes at a time, he would then warm his hands in his armpits until the pain of their re-warming had passed, then continue to sketch. Back at the ship he worked up these sketches into finished pencil drawings and later into water-colours. In this way he secured some extra-ordinary images, including the first accurate images of the Aurora Australis. Ted's colour memorisation technique came into its own in the Antarctic. His colleagues marvelled at the accuracy of his work and the sheer quantity of images that he was able to produce. In addition to his more serious art-work, he also substantially illustrated the ship-board magazine, *The South Polar Times*.

It was during the winter that Scott asked Ted if he would accompany him on the great exploration Southward the following season. The journey did not have the Pole as its objective but was an exploration to the South to see what was there, although, of course, no-one would have complained if the Pole fell into their laps. Everyone aboard hoped for the chance. Ted was astonished to be asked and not entirely happy to be taken away from his biological work; yet he was quietly pleased to be given such an honour. He persuaded Scott to take one other person and Scott chose Shackleton. Once a Spring scurvy outbreak aboard delayed their departure, however, they knew, even before they left the ship, that there was no chance of the Pole. Ted obtained some notes on scurvy and started to ponder its true cause.

Instead of finding a flat icy plain all the way to the South, the Southern party came across magnificent new coastline and mountain ranges. The optimism of the first part of their journey was soon tempered by the rapid failure of the sled-dogs and the need to relay their supplies. Ted dissected one casualty to find that it had died from a form of dysentery. After 60 days of sledging, the men commenced symptoms of scurvy and the dogs were nearly done. It was time to head home. They had achieved a farthest South of 82°. Scott named the inlet at their farthest South for Shackleton and the Cape for Wilson. With the dogs nearly all dead they man-hauled their sledge home. Shackleton was deteriorating rapidly, coughing blood and suffering fainting spells. Scott and Ted, themselves suffering, struggled to get the party home. It was a close call but they made it. A large dinner was held to celebrate their arrival but the stomachs of the three hungry men were so shrunken that they spent all night alternately eating and throwing up. Ted noted that he only had a bath after 3 months sledging out of a sense of duty to his shipmates, such was the pain involved in bathing his bruised and sunburned body. Shackleton's health was deemed to be unreliable and he was evacuated home aboard the relief ship.

Shackleton, Scott and Wilson returned from Farthest South, 2 February 1903

As soon as he was able, Ted worked up the many dozens of sketches from their Southern journey and caught up on his zoological work. Topographical pictures, water-colours of parhelia, mock suns, fog bows and other astonishing visual phenomena of Antarctic sledging, started to emerge from Ted's cabin. It was in the execution of these that Ted's study of Turner started to truly come into its own. His application of the technique of halation was used to great effect in recording the boundaries between ice and light. Ted passed much of the second winter in executing such pictures. *Discovery's* second year in the South was an unexpected bonus. The unrelenting ice had obliged them to remain through not releasing the ship during the summer months. However, it gave Scott the unique opportunity to assess the results of the first year's geographical and scientific work and to plan for a second season to fill in gaps. To Ted, it gave the chance of being the first to study the breeding biology of the Emperor Penguin.

The biology of the Emperor Penguin was, at this time, completely unknown. Therefore it was a cause of considerable excitement when a party, under Lieut. Skelton, found the first breeding rookery of Emperor Penguins at Cape Crozier. Ted had been frustrated not to have had the opportunity to study these but the unexpected second season allowed him to do just this. He left for Cape Crozier as early in the Spring as he dared, in order to secure good specimens of Emperor Penguin eggs. Instead, to his astonishment, he found quite well grown chicks and was led to conclude that these remarkable birds had to lay their eggs in the middle of the Antarctic winter. It was one of a series of remarkable field observations that Ted made of these birds over the following months.

Weddell Seal plate, 'Discovery' expedition report, 1907

To everyone's delight, towards the end of the second summer, the ice finally freed *Discovery*. The Admiralty had sent two relief vessels to evacuate *Discovery* in the event of the ice trapping them again but no-one had wanted to abandon the ship. The Expedition returned in triumph to New Zealand and civilisation and there Ted found Ory waiting for him. The scientific and geographical discoveries of the Expedition were considerable. Additionally, what was to be the last of the great naval expeditions of exploration in the Victorian style had achieved an astonishing visual record of Antarctica, in no small part due to Ted's work aboard.

Cheltenham College Chapel from Westal windows

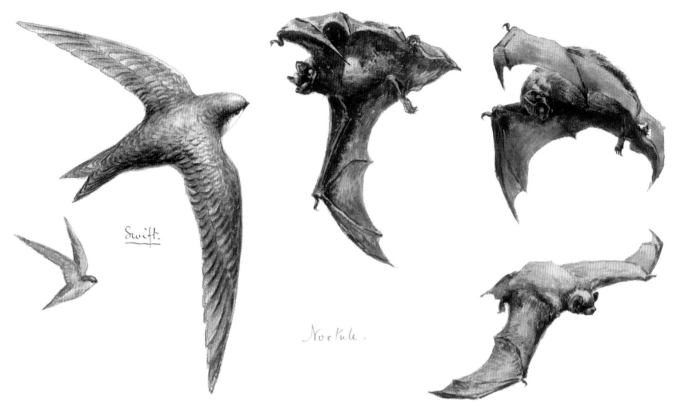

PART II: 1904-1912

"When at last one picks out, from the number of animals and birds one has seen, that aspect which by preference one knows best, then whatever its attitude may be or whatever it may be doing there is in the drawing a grain or two from every animal of the same kind one has ever seen." EAW

Ireland: 1905

The return of the British National Antarctic Expedition to the United Kingdom was greeted with wide acclaim and an almost endless series of dinners. Despite the social whirl, Ted was soon hard at work preparing for the public exhibition of the Expedition's achievements. This opened at the Bruton Gallery in London on 7 November 1904 and was so popular that it subsequently toured many provincial towns. One of the key attractions was Ted's paintings. For the first time in his life Ted found fame, which he disliked and shrank from at every opportunity. Nor did he enjoy the commercialisation of his work. He had innocently agreed to produce copies of his paintings for a modest price out of deference to the Royal Geographical Society which had put up the Expedition. However, he was subsequently persuaded by the director of the Bruton Gallery to allow them to sell these copies for a considerably greater price, from which the gallery took a handsome commission, of course. Over 80 orders were placed which Ted diligently executed at his home in Bushey over the next six months but he received a good deal of trouble and little of the 20-30 guinea picture price (approx. £1500-£2000 today) for his efforts. He was, in essence, thoroughly fleeced and with no room for legal redress.

Nevertheless, the exhibition brought Ted to the attention of numerous individuals. Many visitors to the exhibition were impressed by his landscape and topographical work. What was truly surprising to the visiting crowds, however, was the 'aliveness' of his studies of the birds and animals. This was, at the time, unusual. Sir Joseph Hooker, who had sailed with Captain James Clark Ross in a similar position to that of Ted with Scott, made his admiration for Ted's work in this regard widely known. They later met and Ted studied Hooker's Antarctic portfolio. Ted was also pleased to meet the artists Hubert von Herkomer and J.Swan, and to renew his acquaintance with the Duchess of Bedford, whom he had known as a girl. She now took him under her wing and gave him the run of the Woburn estate. Other significant meetings included one with the Murray brothers, who would, years later, publish Ted's biography. They encouraged him to write and illustrate for a living. Hallam Murray, who also painted, offered Ted a critique of his work, "correcting several faults which run through all of my painting". He was delighted. This was exactly the sort of artistic exchange that Ted sought as some compensation for his lack of art lessons. These he still craved but, if anything, had even less time for now than ever before. It also encouraged him in his aspiration to write and illustrate wildlife books. He was particularly keen on producing something "inspired by" the work of William J. Long and of Ernest Thompson-Seton, whose illustrated tales of animals had been such a success.

Edward and Oriana Wilson with family members at The Crippetts, c.1905

Ted was additionally pursuing an idea at this time to return to New Zealand and become something along the lines of a "government scientist" as Thompson-Seton was in Canada. He and Ory had fallen in love with New Zealand during the *Discovery*'s comings and goings there and longed to return. Ted had been shocked by the rapid disappearance of the native New Zealand bush and its associated wildlife, particularly the birds, and he wanted the chance to go and live there in order to record and study the vanishing species before they disappeared. He wrote to numerous officials offering to work essentially for his and Ory's keep in order to achieve this but did not receive an encouraging response. However, most of these ideas of Ted's slowly started to disappear as practical options. As his mountain of work grew around him, he had scant opportunity to write his animal tales or to return to New Zealand. Instead, Ted undertook to write and illustrate the reports on birds and mammals for the *Discovery* expedition reports. This resulted in being employed for four days a week at the Natural History Museum, working with eminent zoologists on the Expedition collections. Ted wanted his monograph on the Emperor Penguin to become a classic. He also undertook work for books connected with the Expedition, in particular Captain Scott's own book *The Voyage of the Discovery*, a facsimile of *The South Polar Times* and the Expedition's *Album of Photographs and Sketches*. It was 1908 before he had completed the numerous publication and illustrative projects that arose from the Expedition. These projects helped to keep him in regular contact with Captain Scott and introduced them both to Mr. and Mrs. Reginald Smith of the publishers, Smith, Elder and Co.. They were to become close personal friends.

Ted and Ory managed to escape his increasing work load to spend Christmas with the Wilson family in Cheltenham. Although his mother had by now given up the lease on *The Crippetts*, Ted still liked to walk up to the farm and to visit its woods and hedgerows. It was a special pleasure that Ted liked to indulge in and which became rarer as his success grew. Apart from anything else, Ted was much in demand as a lecturer and delighted his audiences with tales and impressions of penguins. He also began to campaign for the protection of penguins, which were being boiled for their oil in increasing numbers. He gave papers on the subject before the R.S.P.B. and the International Ornithological Congress. It started a process which finally met with success many years after Ted's death.

It was after addressing the British Ornithologists Union at the Restaurant Friscati in March 1905 that Ted was introduced to Lord Lovat. W.R.Ogilvie-Grant had invited Lord Lovat to attend the meeting especially to meet Ted. He was the Chairman of the Board of Agriculture's Inquiry on the investigation of Grouse Disease. The Board of Agriculture had commenced the Inquiry because grouse shooting was an important part of the rural economy and the birds were dying of a mysterious disease. The cause had so far eluded researchers. Lord Lovat was looking for a new field naturalist who was also a bacteriologist and doctor to carry out the field-work for the Inquiry. This contract was expected to engage the person concerned for six months of the year. Ogilvie-Grant thought that Ted was the perfect candidate. Upon meeting him, Lord Lovat was so impressed that he invited Ted to Carlisle the following day to a meeting of gamekeepers who were to discuss the subject. Ted agreed and after attending the Carlisle meeting accepted the post of Field Observer to the Commission.

Additional offers of work kept pouring in. Of particular excitement was contact from an old Cambridge friend, Gerald Barrett-Hamilton, who was a keen admirer of Ted's work. Barrett-Hamilton had been engaged to produce a new edition of Bell's *A History of British Mammals* and he wanted Ted to do the illustrations. Ted jumped at the chance, the thought of illustrating many of the animals of the British countryside, which he knew so well, was hugely appealing. Shortly after he had agreed to this Ted was contacted by the ornithologist Eagle Clarke who had been commissioned to produce a new edition of Yarrell's *A History of British Birds*. He, too, wanted Ted to provide the illustrations. Ted was overjoyed; the chance to illustrate all 350 species of British birds was a project that was so close to his heart that he simply could not refuse. Since the grouse work was only scheduled to take up six months of his year, Ted was confident that he could meet all of these other demands in the six months remaining to him.

Before these projects began in earnest, however, a plan had been hatched by Ted's parents for a full family holiday in the West of Ireland. The Wilson family had a tradition of such holidays, during which the time would be spent largely in picnicking, reading, sketching and natural history collecting. It was to be the last such family holiday, although this wasn't realised at the time. Despite his parents instruction that it was to be a total holiday, such were the demands on Ted that he nevertheless took unfinished work with him to complete. His parents had taken a house for the month of August, at the appropriately named *Sketchers Cottage* in a wild corner of Kerry overlooking Dingle Bay. The remoteness of the area at this time meant that it was alive with wildlife, including many species that were already quite rare on the British mainland. The skies were still full of Choughs, Red Kites, Ravens and waders. The party were greatly excited to spot Grey Seals basking on the rocks not long after their arrival and Ted, with Ory, spent many quiet hours watching and sketching them playing in the surf. Many of the sketches that he made at this time were of immediate use as preparatory material for his illustrations of the British birds and mammals. He also produced a series of landscapes. George Seaver, who many years later was to be Ted's biographer, thought these to be amongst his finest works, exuding "the charm and glamour of the 'Celtic twilight'". Ted was relaxed when he painted them, something that he rarely had time for with his painting again. He had gained a great deal of experience as an artist since the last time that he had painted for relaxation and he revelled in the freedom to indulge these skills

whilst at ease on the beach. Most of their time was spent sketching, or reading, although Ted and Ory did manage a visit to nearby Killarney. It was a wonderful, tranquil few weeks.

On the return journey to England, Ted left the main family party in order to take the chance to visit Barrett-Hamilton, who lived in Waterford. They discussed illustrations for the forthcoming book and Ted made use of the opportunity to visit and sketch some of the castles and abbeys of the Irish South-east. Once back in England, it was time to knuckle down and produce results for the numerous projects in which he was now engaged.

"Seals!" Edward and Oriana Wilson seal spotting with family members.
Ireland, August 1905

Mus sylvaticus celticus

from Kerry

Ireland: 1905

"A happy life is not built up of tours abroad and pleasant holidays, but of little clumps of violets noticed by the roadside, hidden away almost so that only those can see them who have God's peace and love in their hearts; in one long continuous chain of little joys; little whispers from the spiritual world; little gleams of sunshine on our daily work... So long as I have stuck to Nature and the New Testament I have only got happier and happier every day."
EAW

Dingle Bay from Ardroe, Inch – Aug. 25. 1905.

Ireland: 1905

Anascaul River.
above Ballynan.

Aug. 20. 1905.

Ireland: 1905

McGillycuddy's Reeks.

"I want to write, and I want to draw, only I want to spend a year or two at least in <u>learning</u> how to draw, because the more I draw and sketch the more hopeless I feel about ever being anything more than an amateur and a dabbler... I not only have never been taught, but I have never, even once, <u>seen</u> anyone at work who knew how to do things... I shall always hope to get this training some day, for in painting I am quite sure it is never too late to learn..." EAW

MacGillicuddy Reeks.

Aug. 25. 1905.

Sanderling.
Inch. Anascaul.
Co. Kerry.

Ringed Plover.
Inch, Anascaul. Aug. 25. 1905.

Legs, feet bright orange red. Black nails.

Redshank.
Inch mud flats.
Aug. 25. 1905.

Knot.
Anascaul. Kerry.
Aug. 30. 1905.

"My little bird-pictures are just visible proofs of my love for them, and attempts to praise God and bring others to love Him through His works..." EAW

Curlew.   life size.
Aug. 26. 1905.
Inch, Anascaul. Kerry.

Feet & legs black.
with a fourth toe.

Inch Sands.
Anascaul Co. Kerry.
Aug. 10. 1905.

Feet & legs dull ochre yellowish grey.
No fourth hind toe.

Ringed Plover.
Aug. 26. 1905.

Inch Sands.
Anascaul, Kerry.

Ireland: 1905

Brandon Head - & Carrigaghanoe Pt

St. Brendan's birthplace - Fenit Harbour.

Ireland: 1905

McGillycuddy's Reeks. from Inch. Sand Dunes.

"...how hard it is to live and how hard it is to die. Isn't it a puzzle? And yet what a fund of joy there is in life all the same... I sometimes think that Time is the only thing that prevents this life from being absolute heaven." EAW

Killarney Mts from Anascaul Road.

Ireland: 1905

Looking to Cromane from Inch

Killarney
1904

Feet & legs dark orange. Black nails.

Mus hibernicus.

Nov. 21. 05.   Waterford.

Turnstone.
Aug. 26. 1905.

Inch Sands. Anascaul. Kerry.

Exact size.

Curlew.

Grey Seal. Dingle Bay. Ireland. Aug. 1905.

"[Grey Seals] feeding on the incoming tide. Rising every 5 minutes to breathe and look around, about 200 yards from the water's edge; seemed to feed amongst weed covered rocks. Watched one working up the coast for eight hours one day. Other days one or two were always to be seen about 10 a.m. off the rocks or off the sandy shore lying amongst the breakers. Sometimes as many as 25 have been seen out together on a spit of rock at low tide. Also in the caves along this coast." EAW

Head of a fish called "Lahen" by the Irish. Very much like a Seatrout. Anascaul River. Aug. 24. 1905.

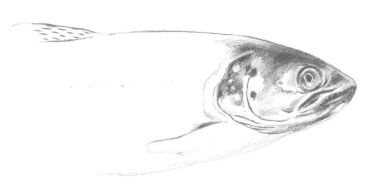

Ireland: 1905

Blarney Castle Ireland.

Ireland: 1905

"... I must by degrees write out an all-embracing song of thanksgiving and praise which shall include the Willow Warblers, and Cole-tits as well as the budding green of the Beech-mast and the Birch catkins..." EAW

The Grouse Disease Inquiry: 1905-1910

Ted's work as the Field Observer to the Grouse Disease Inquiry soon started in earnest. By early 1906 there were dead grouse "pouring in by every post" to the Wilson home at Bushey. Every dead grouse found on a British moor was dispatched to Ted for examination and a good many were suffering from delays in transit. Over the course of the Inquiry he would dissect just under 2,000 birds, leading one of his colleagues to comment that in whatever location Ted was situated he was constantly surrounded "by a halo of grouse feathers and unravelled entrails". This was not terribly popular in station hotels. As he travelled around the country in pursuit of his work, odious remains were occasionally forgotten. The vast majority of the grouse sent to him he turned into museum skins, as well as taking detailed biological notes. Every bird then had a report filed upon it. Upon filing one such report on a brace of grouse recently received through the post, Ted received the astonished reply that they had been intended for him to eat, not to dissect. In all of this work Ted received the competent support of Ory, who was, to all intents and purposes, his unpaid assistant.

The Inquiry was very complex and fraught with politics. Every landowner, sportsman and ghillie was convinced of their own expertise regarding the true cause of the epidemics. Additionally, there had been two predecessors to Ted in the post of Field Observer, including the respected scientist, Professor Klein; both had put forward theories on the disease. Added to this potent cocktail was the fact that Ted no longer believed in blood sports. Although he had hunted in his youth and was a good shot, Ted had ceased to believe that blood sports had any place in a civilised society. Likewise, he had long since given up his egg collecting activities except for strictly scientific purposes and now preferred to simply draw or paint live birds and their nests. These were unusual views in the Edwardian era and Ted rather wisely chose to rarely express his views on blood sport in his current undertaking. However, he was less hesitant to give his opinion on the treatment of 'vermin' on the grouse moors or on the likely or unlikely causes of grouse disease. Many a ghillie took affront to these views until they started to realise that Ted knew as much, or more, of the habits of grouse and their predators as they did. Such conversations were often held whilst strolling over the grouse moors where Ted often outpaced these professional keepers, much to their surprise. One way or another, Ted slowly won them around and whilst they might not end up agreeing with him he earned their respect. This was critical to the success of the Inquiry, over the course of which Ted visited most of the major grouse moors of Scotland and many in northern England.

In July 1906 Ted and Ory moved up to Scotland to be nearer to the grouse work. Lord Lovat put his shooting lodge at Glendoe at their disposal and they frequently stayed here during the Inquiry. Ted rapidly made friends with the monks of the nearby monastery of St. Benedict and with many of the other local landowners. He executed landscapes whenever he was able, although the Scottish landscapes are few in number as he was so busy with other work. Nevertheless, he continued the process of his artistic self-tuition, experimenting with a different water-colour technique whilst in Scotland. Ted generally utilised a technique of painting on damp, thin paper which allows for delicate colour blending but has to be carried out quickly. He started to experiment with the use of a dry, rough paper; however, he soon abandoned this in favour of his old method.

Edward and Oriana Wilson in Scotland

Despite the fact that grouse were continuing to arrive in the post, none had yet arrived with the dreaded disease. In fact it took 3 years before an outbreak of the disease occurred again. Ted's suspicion as to the cause of grouse disease had started to fall upon a minute threadworm which he had found infecting the cœca of weaker birds and appeared to interrupt the digestive process, so killing the bird. It was of considerable delight to Ted, therefore, to discover the worm alive and wriggling in a diseased grouse lung, to watch them hatching and burrowing in the gut and to find dead worms in the liver. He was getting close to being able to prove that the threadworm was indeed the cause of the grouse disease. Ted rapidly traced the mode of infection to the dew drops on the tips of the young shoots upon which the grouse feed. It took him many early mornings of study upon the moors to gather the evidence for this but he revelled in it. Ted was rarely indoors except when examining grouse or working with his co-workers upon the microscopic examination of organisms. They were searching for the secondary host, in order to give a complete account of the life of the threadworm and the course of the epidemic disease. However, the secondary host proved somewhat elusive. One hotel even had a bag of suspect slugs left behind in it when Ted rushed for a train. He dreaded to think what the chambermaid thought.

The Grouse Disease Inquiry was taking ever increasing amounts of Ted's time and far more than the six months per year that he had been led to expect. He often had to travel from one end of the country to the other for meetings or to visit grouse moors, the owners of which often entertained him so well that it "cuts into my work". He often spent his train journeys catching up on proof corrections or correspondence. He had no time for reading and so, often as not, Ory would read out loud to him whilst he was dissecting grouse. With the expansion of the grouse work Ted was seriously over-committed and as a result became severely over-worked. Yet he dealt with the many demands upon him with a typically calm assiduousness, doing each and every thing in front of him without fuss and to the best of his ability. He was determined to explain the cause of the grouse disease and equally determined that each and every plate for the mammals and the birds should be a unique composition based, wherever possible, on his personal observation.

In February 1907 an unexpected letter arrived from Shackleton informing Ted that he was heading back to the Antarctic with his own expedition and with the objective of reaching the South Pole. He wanted Ted to be his second in command. Ted declined, due to the fact that he was already over-committed and really did not feel that he could leave the grouse work. Ted also wrote to Lord Lovat re-affirming his commitment to seeing the work through. Shackleton failed in his attempts to extricate Ted from the Inquiry. These letters were followed several weeks later by letters from Scott, who was upset that Shackleton had announced that he was going to use his old base without consulting him. Scott was also brewing plans for another expedition. Both men turned to Ted to mediate in their dispute and a deal was brokered. Shackleton eventually failed to keep it and when he returned to the United Kingdom in 1909 as a hero, Ted broke off their friendship.

An additional shock occurred when Ted had his suitcase stolen at Glasgow station. It contained all the results of his grouse work to date. Ted was deeply upset but set about salvaging what he could from his original rough notes. It was a huge amount of additional work that Ted could have done without. At this time the Inquiry was studying the effectiveness of rotational burning of the moors to control the spread of bracken and perhaps of the threadworm.

In September 1907, Ted and Ory finally managed to have a few days of rest. They were invited to *Burnside,* the shooting-bungalow of their friends the Reginald Smiths at Cortachy, Kirriemuir. Captain Scott was staying too and, as Ted had already agreed to head South with him once more, they started to formulate plans for the next Antarctic expedition. Ted and Ory stayed at Cortachy again for much of the following summer. They had also taken a house in Cambridge where during the months that he wasn't on the moors, Ted was carrying out laboratory work on the grouse disease. He carried out experiments on living grouse, infecting them with the threadworm in order to prove the cause of the disease. For this he required a Vivisector's License, much to the Wilson family's amusement.

Mr. & Mrs Reginald Smith, Oriana Wilson and Captain Scott. Cortachy, 1907

By mid-1909 Ted had been publicly confirmed as the Chief of Scientific Staff for Scott's forthcoming Expedition. Expedition preparations started to be added to Ted's long list of work. He was also trying hard to finish the grouse work before heading South. Of the final report of the Inquiry, Ted wrote approximately one third and provided the majority of the illustrations. A paper promised to the Zoological Society on the changes of plumage in Red Grouse, was written on the train and finished in a station waiting-room. He was so tired that he took to working standing up, so that he didn't fall asleep over his work. Ted was still trying to finish the grouse work when he sailed South in June 1910. The final instalments were posted home to the Inquiry from South Africa in August. The grouse work was completed at last.

Ted was destined never to see the results of his work in the final report of the Inquiry. However, The Grouse Disease Inquiry was the first major study to investigate fluctuations in numbers in a bird species and stood for almost a century as the most extensive scientific investigation carried out into a disease in a wild bird population. For his part in it Ted was later recognised as being amongst the world's leading ornithologists for the first part of the Twentieth Century.

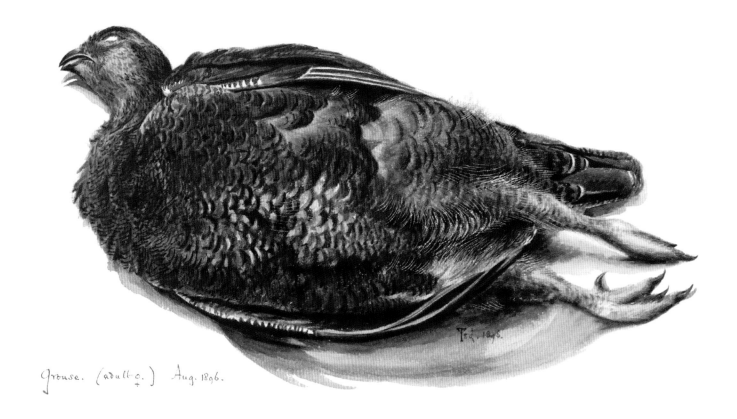

Grouse. (adult ♂) Aug. 1896.

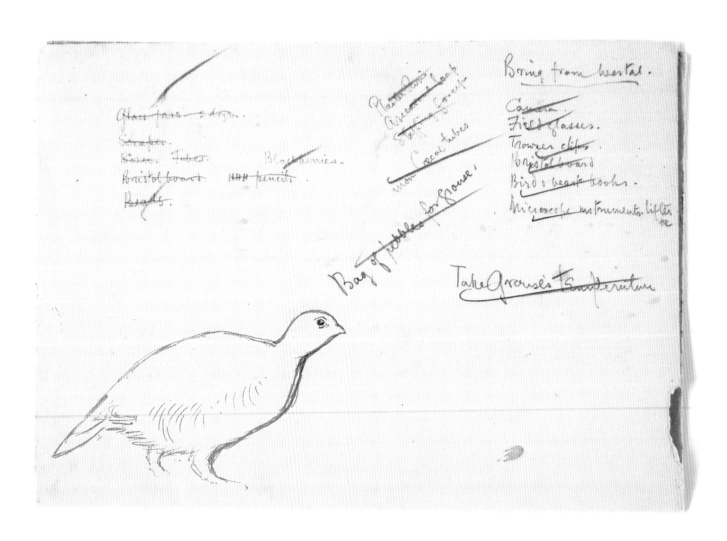

*"... turned out at 4 a.m. ... - Black game bubbling
and Grouse a'becking..." EAW*

Red Grouse.

The Grouse Disease Inquiry: 1905-1910

"If the place were mine I should kill nothing except for painting and helping others and myself to get to know things better. I think that is right... The love of sport is very strong in the English, and it wants a long and intimate friendship with birds and animals to feel unable to enjoy it. There are birds and beasts that I know so well and like so well that I don't think I should kill them for anybody... But when you see six or eight stoats hunting down a family of little fluffy yellow-brown grouse chicks, and the mother grouse in such a state because she can't help them, you feel you ought to shoot the stoats; but if you like stoats as I do it goes against the grain." EAW

Pl. XIII.
(P.Z.S. 1910. *Pl. XCIII.*)

FEET OF RED GROUSE: (1) NEW WINTER-FEATHERS AND NAILS; (2) FULL WINTER-PLUMAGE;
(3) (4) (5) and (6) SHOWING STAGES IN MOULTING OF NAILS.

XIII. Grouse, red type, feet showing winter-plumage.
    Fig. 1. Right foot showing new winter-feathers and new nails (No. 1177).
     ,, 2. Left foot showing full-feathered winter-plumage.
Feet of grouse, showing replacement of nails.
    Fig. 3. Right foot (No. 1148) with old nails ready to be shed.
     ,, 4.   ,,   ,, in median vertical section.
     ,, 5. Left ,, (No. 1167). 5a, old nails; 5b, new nails; 5c, shed nails.
     ,, 6. Right ,, (No. 1185) with new feathers and new nails.

The Grouse Disease Inquiry: 1905-1910

"The chief rock that lies in my path is the possibility of an outbreak of Grouse disease; if that happens I am bound to go straight to it by the next train to investigate it and there is literally no one who can take my place." EAW

Pl. XII.
(P.Z.S. 1910. *Pl. XC.*)

Andre & Sleigh, Ltd

FEMALE GROUSE, RED TYPE ; FEATHERS FROM FLANKS.

Female grouse, red type, feathers from flanks.   Natural size.

Fig. *a* and *c* (from No. 1864), *g* and *h* (from No. 226), and *k* (from No. 632), are varieties of the spring flank-feathers.

Fig. *b* (from No. 575) is a flank-feather from a very black hen.

Fig. *d* from No. 1864) is an example of what is termed fine-barred, dark-red winter-plumage, with narrow black bars or lines on rather dark rufous chestnut, the latter being slightly bleached towards the tip.

Figs. *e* and *f* (from No. 1864) and *l* and *m* (from No. 664) illustrate intermediate stages of colouration, the feathers probably having broken through the skin when winter-conditions prevailed, and having completed their growth under summer-conditions.

Figs. *i* and *n* (from No. 664) illustrate the reasoning upon which is based the view just mentioned ; of these two feathers there is no doubt that *n* was being grown much later than *i*, and therefore more in summer-conditions, producing summer breeding-plumage.

The Grouse Disease Inquiry: 1905-1910

Views near Fort Augustus

The Grouse Disease Inquiry: 1905-1910

"I went out again alone first up Glenmarkie, then to the right into a beautiful wild corrie where a Golden Eagle's nest had been built in an accessible cliff. I got to it and found it quite freshly added to - tufts of fresh heather, a sod of turf - many newly shed eagle-feathers and freshly eaten Grouse remains besides droppings." EAW

Views near Fort Augustus

The Grouse Disease Inquiry: 1905-1910

Black Grouse -

*"Black game at night
make a noise something
between a pigeon
and an owl."*
EAW

Loch Ness at Fort Augustus

The Grouse Disease Inquiry: 1905-1910

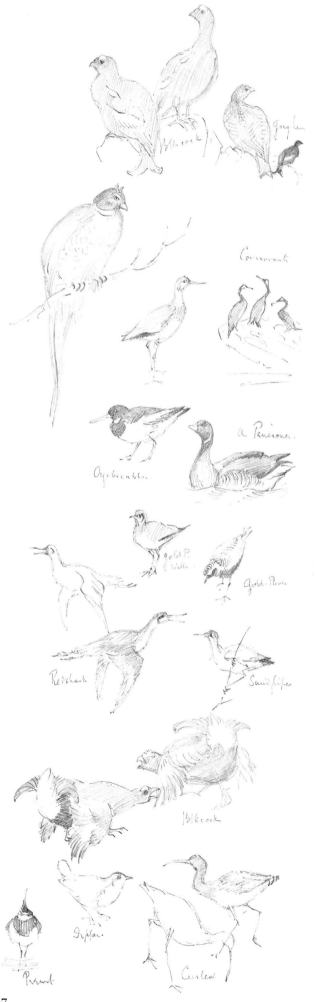

"Left Cortachy at 10.30 p.m., walking into Glenclova as far as the Blackgame wood, but a wind sprang up which prevented any dew-fall... There were no fewer than 7 Corncrakes craking all night between Kirriemuir and Burnside. Besides these, Curlew, Peewit, and Tawny Owl were the night-birds most in evidence... On way back to Kirriemuir saw Snipe, Golden Plover, Curlew, Common and Blackhead Gull and Blackbacked lesser, many Brown Hares, Pheasants and Partridges. Greenfinches abundant along roadside, all feeding on Dandelion seed. Got back 6 a.m." EAW

The Grouse Disease Inquiry: 1905-1910

The Kirk, Fort Augustus

Landscape, near Fort Augustus

The Grouse Disease Inquiry: 1905-1910

"My old beliefs are all every atom as strong as ever. It isn't that any of my convictions or any of my longings have altered or died out; it is that they are out of sight only, as the foundations of a house are out of sight, but they are there for as long as the building lasts, and they are quite sound. I am reminded of the Fort Augustus Chapel of the Monastery. Once foundations are laid they should be built on, and the more they are built on the more they disappear from view. If ever you see signs of the foundations giving way, then tell me it is time to stop building..."

EAW

Frontispiece.

(P.Z.S. 1910. *Pl. LXXVIII.*)

Andre & Sleigh, Ltd.

PAIR OF RED GROUSE IN SUMMER WITH YOUNG CHICKS.

The Grouse Disease Inquiry: 1905-1910

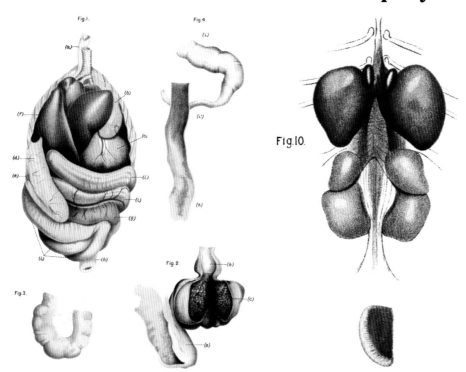

Plate Details from *The Grouse in Health and in Disease*

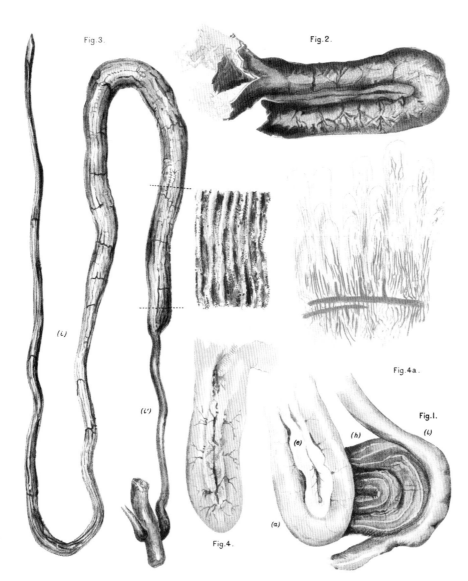

"I have just discovered the living young threadworm alive and wriggling in diseased lung as well as dead ones in the liver. We had before seen the worms hatching from the threadworm eggs in the gut and ulceration caused there by their burrowing, so we have really got the whole thing if Seligman can corroborate Klein's opinion that the lung trouble is due to bacilli of coli communis group. If this is so obviously the worms have carried them to the lung from the gut... This is my view. I have been letting Shipley and Seligman know all I have found and am waiting to hear their objections." EAW

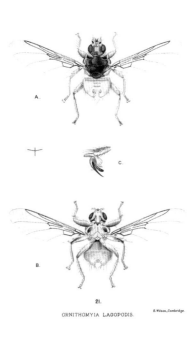

ORNITHOMYIA LAGOPODIS.

The British Mammals: 1905-1910

Shortly after his return from the British National Antarctic Expedition, Ted and Ory settled in Bushey. For a couple of years this proved to be an ideal base, not only due to its proximity to London and the countryside but because Bushey is a centre for artists. At this point in time this was largely due to the residence of Hubert von Herkomer, who had opened the Herkomer Art School in Bushey in 1883 and cocked a snoop at traditional methods of art teaching. His progressive methods produced a number of successful artists and attracted students from all over the world. From 1905 the Life School was run by one of Herkomer's most successful pupils, Lucy Kemp-Welch, a noted painter of horses. Ted and Ory dined with Herkomer and got on well with him. Ted subsequently attended the Life School and reputedly executed some striking studies of horses. However, it is unclear in what capacity he was there, or for how long. It must be presumed that he exchanged ideas on the execution of such drawings with Kemp-Welch and other artists and that he further developed his own technique through any criticism received but it seems doubtful that he was a pupil as such. If he was, it was a brief course. Such details have been lost and the whereabouts of his horse drawings are no longer known. If Ted had intended to go to Art School at Bushey and fulfil his lifetime's dream of art lessons then it seems odd that this isn't recorded. In any case the dream was not fulfilled to any extent; his work simply took over his life. Nevertheless, the experience must have been helpful to him in his continuing self-development as an artist and in the subsequent execution of his mammal pictures. A member of the school, Alfred Soord, subsequently painted Ted's portrait and they struck up an agreeable friendship. The portrait was exhibited in the Royal Academy Exhibition of 1910.

Edward Wilson c.1910

After his discussions with Barrett-Hamilton in Waterford, Ted headed back to Bushey and set to work on the illustrations for the British mammal book throughout the autumn of 1905. He paid a three day visit to Mr. Cocks at Henley where he produced over 70 sketches of the Pine Martens, Wild Cats, Badgers and Otters, which were kept there. Ted was determined that, wherever possible, every plate should be produced from his personal observation of the live animal. His preparatory sketching was often carried out in the field but he also sketched specimens that were easily accessible in private collections or at the London Zoo. This was particularly welcome for species that he was unlikely to encounter in the field. He could also be found studying British mammal skins in the Natural History Museum or at home, for it wasn't merely specimens of dead grouse that arrived in the post. When news of his mammal work with Barrett-Hamilton spread, amateur enthusiasts sent him their dead mammal specimens for painting and study. However, Ted continued in his search for live specimens. He visited the estate at Woburn and was delighted to study so many species in semi-wild surroundings. In February 1906, he returned to his friend Mr. Cocks and with Mr. Heatley Noble went bat hunting. They entered an old tunnel excavated through a chalk hill and here they found bats of four species, Daubenton's, Natterer's, Whiskered and Long-eared. Ted collected 20 bats and brought them back to Bushey. He was quietly working on one of these live specimens in his studio when a flea crawled out of the bat fur and onto the tip of his pencil. It says much of the breadth of Ted's knowledge of natural history that he instantly recognised it as a rare species that would be appreciated for the collection of Mr. Charles Rothschild. He called out to Ory for assistance and she had to abandon her soufflé in the kitchen in order to fetch a tube of spirit into which the flea could be placed. This incident was later portrayed in the 1949 film, *Scott of the Antarctic*.

Once Ted and Ory moved up to Scotland to work on the Grouse Inquiry, he found new opportunities for executing field studies of mammals, particularly at Glendoe and Cortachy. He hunted bats in the Monastery of St. Benedict and during early morning strolls across the moors would often stop to sketch the mammals that he encountered. Nevertheless, it wasn't always possible for Ted to study a species in the field nor to find good dead specimens on which to base his pictures. This was particularly difficult for British whale species. Ted did study whales in British waters for the mammal book, having the opportunity to do so from the boat crossing during a visit to the grouse moors of Shetland in 1906. However he was not able to study all of the cetacean species that he needed to illustrate, and utilised a combination of photographs in books, or the field sketches that he had made of cetacea whilst aboard *Discovery*. These sketches were exactly what he wanted, being studies of the live animal, but led to a rather amusing error in the plate of the Killer Whale, for here he has clearly painted an Antarctic Killer Whale rather than a British Killer Whale. They are the same species, of course, and Ted presumed that they must look the same but there is clear visual difference of which he was obviously unaware. In the Antarctic the back patch of the Killer Whale is a deep yellow, due to the diatoms that grow upon them in those waters, whilst it is a more normal white in the British Killer Whale. A quick look at the preparatory sketches upon which the plate is based confirms the source of the mistake. It is an error by which he would have been heartily amused, had anyone realised. Ted did realise, however, that the cetacea were the weakest point of his mammal work. In 1910, shortly before sailing South aboard *Terra Nova,* he visited the Shetlands once again. This visit was specifically to spend two weeks whaling in and around the Shetland Islands aboard a Norwegian whaling vessel. The visit had a dual purpose: both to prepare himself for whale work in the Antarctic and to improve his whale material for the mammal book. Whilst he left Barrett-Hamilton with finished plates when he sailed South, he hoped to have a chance to re-work the cetacea images upon his return from the Antarctic, since this volume was due to be the last published.

Both Ted and Barrett-Hamilton set themselves high standards for the mammal book. In this regard, as in many others, their lives paralleled one another. They both attended the same lectures at Cambridge, used the same laboratories and finished equal in the Tripos. They were both candidates for the scientific staff aboard *Discovery* but Ted won out on that occasion. However, Barrett-Hamilton wrote the chapter on the seals for the *Antarctic Manual,* and so essentially wrote Ted his instructions for the seal work aboard *Discovery.* After the Bruton Gallery exhibition, Barrett-Hamilton was most keen to secure Ted's services for the illustration of his book and it is as well that they already had such a good working relationship, for Barrett-Hamilton was a ruthless critic of Ted's work, something that Ted was very grateful for. As Barrett-Hamilton recalled: "…it was sometimes necessary to call him to earth for a demonstration on murine osteology but no man ever took criticism in better part. As a rule he forestalled it by a genial counter attack:- 'You are so polite this morning that I know you are going to tear my drawings to pieces' was his typical opening…"

Barrett-Hamilton drew the best out of Ted and thought him a genius. Others were equally impressed by his mammal paintings. The publishers Oliver and Boyd showed a sketch of a Stoat to Eagle Clarke and Grimshaw and were told that Millais couldn't do anything as good. Ted was astonished: "…this is of course humbug but they took it in and congratulated me most heartily, so I have something to live up to now." Others were particularly impressed by the work that he produced in a blue and grey wash for the black and white illustrations in the mammal book. The plates were designed to meet the publication requirements of the day; indeed, Ted often produced several versions of the same plate for the client to choose from in order to satisfy their requirements. Yet, widely acclaimed as they were, his illustrations were ahead of the technical possibilities of his time. Barrett-Hamilton was to regret that publication had diminished the colours of his images. In comparison, Ted's original preparatory work is as fresh and alive as if it had been drawn yesterday. Had he been able to advance beyond both the technical and the aesthetic restrictions with which he had to work, he might have left a somewhat different illustrative legacy.

Nevertheless, published in parts from 1910 to 1921, *A History of British Mammals* by Barrett-Hamilton and illustrated by Edward Wilson became a classic work on the British mammals. It is still sought after and was republished as recently as 1978. This is perhaps especially surprising since it was never completed and so many of Ted's plates were never used. In particular Volume III on the marine mammals was never produced. The first part was issued in October 1910, shortly after Ted had sailed South aboard *Terra Nova* but he never saw the finished work. Nor was he to have the opportunity to re-paint the cetacea. Having sent a batch of illustrations back from South Africa, he didn't return from the frozen South. Shortly afterwards, Barrett-Hamilton also died in the Antarctic: he had a heart attack in January 1914 upon the island of South Georgia. He was studying the whales.

Edward A. Wilson by A.U.Soord

Red Squirrel

The British Mammals: 1905-1910

"A squirrel then came up - near by tree - passed the hawk and went down another about 20 yards off. The moment it was well below in level, the hawk went for it and apparently got its claws into it, but tumbled over and had to leave it, after much scrabbling, and then flew off down the wood." EAW

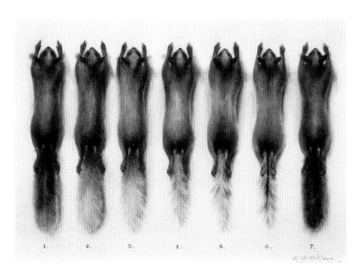

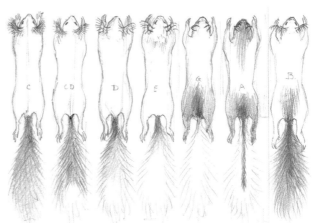

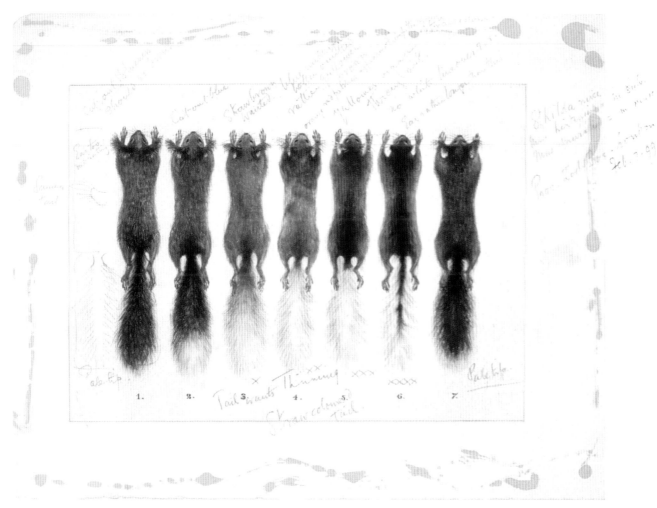

Hedgehog

The British Mammals: 1905-1910

Brown Hare

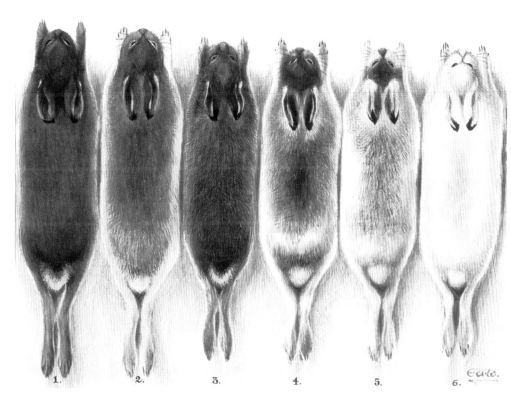

Irish and Scottish Blue Hare skins

"First birds waking just as light began to show, about 3 a.m., were Peewits and Skylarks. Every Skylark burst into song at once. Then Partridges, and a Blackbird, and then a Hare came and looked at me, and then all the world awoke and I followed suit. I found a baby Hare, not much bigger than my fist, lying in a tiny form domed over with dead tussock grass, so that it was almost invisible from above, and I thought it was a hawk sitting on a nest. It was prettily marked, and had a pure white blaze on the forehead: it ran when I handled it. Walked from 4 to 8.30 a.m. when I got home for breakfast. Slept two hours, and painted rest of day." EAW

Noctule Bats

The British Mammals: 1905-1910

Serotine

Myotis nattereri.
ad. ♀.
July 5.06. Bradfield - N° Reading.

Drawn from a dead bat.   Spec. A

"I think it's wonderful how the idea of an animal,- form, colour, character, and even the most unusual surroundings - is all there at last, when one knows the animal well enough - little bits from years and years ago when one first saw the animal in a hedgerow - it's all there ready to come to hand when at last you say, now I am going to paint it." EAW

Black face

Black shoulder patch

Whitish collar.

Barbastelle.

Shrewsbury   Aug. 26. 1905.

Long Eared Bat.

1½ times, life size.   Ears.

Plecotus pipistrellus   Spt. A.

This edge of the ear rarely so cocklikes as here drawn — usually quite straight

Noctule. ♂.

Sept. 7. 1905.

Sent dead from Bowdon by J. A. Coward.

Ventral aspect.

Dorsal aspect.

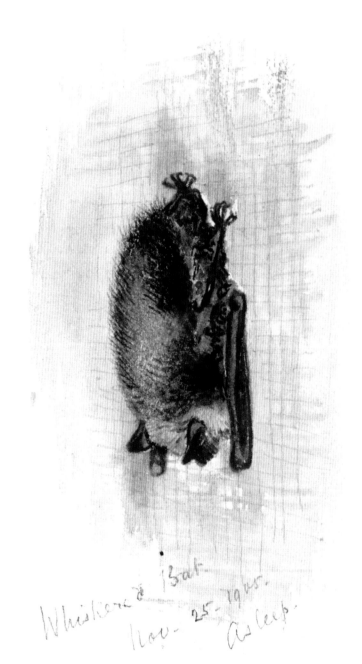

Life size.   * Decidedly paler & more ochreous on the under side of the body.

♂. Shot on Oct. 9. 05 at Copthorne. Sussex.

Rhinolophus hipposideros.

Dec. 1905.

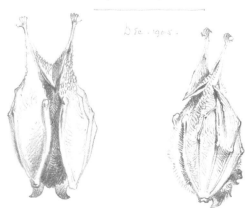

(Asleep - during life)

Asleep - (alive.)

Whiskered Bat.

Nov. 25. 1905.

Asleep.

Pipistrelle Bats

"... my work is endless, it seems as if I could not possibly get through it all and yet bit by bit it gets done." EAW

Jan. 16.02.   Feb. 2.02.   Killer Whale.

Killer Whale

The British Mammals: 1905-1910

Harbour Porpoise

"[The White-beaked Dolphins] spouted under the bows just as I happened to be watching the bow wave. It was strange that four years ago I should have had the rare good fortune to see a school of Caaing whales breeching one after another on this identical journey to Scotland." EAW

Common (Harbour) Seal

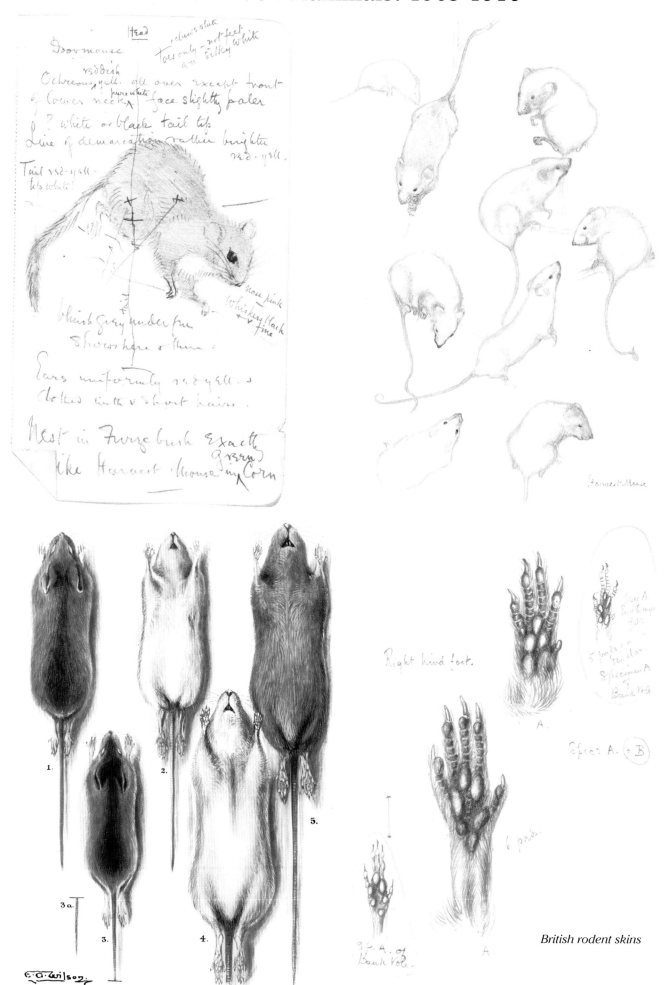

British rodent skins

The British Mammals: 1905-1910

"The keynote of all my longing is to know as much as I can about anything that is still as God made it; I never have the slightest feeling that country rambling is mere amusement or waste of time, it is converse with God through His works. That sounds almost too fine to be true." EAW

Pygmy Shrew

The British Mammals: 1905-1910

The British Mammals: 1905-1910

"Nearly every year there are Cubs in the Earth where in 1884 the young Badger was killed by Bernard and the Elliott's dogs. This is at the top end of the Spain Grip. Any evening one could go and sit on the bank facing this Earth and watch the Cubs at play. Foxes are by no means always night roamers or only to be seen with the hounds. On many occasions I have come on a Fox hunting at midday in the heat of the Summer." EAW

The British Mammals: 1905-1910

Stoats hunting a Rabbit

Mountain Hare, Stoat and Weasel in Winter Pelage

The British Mammals: 1905-1910

Stoat. B

Putorius erminens. ♂
(Summer furs.)

"Stoats more often seen at Crippetts than the Weasel. Two or three may be seen together. Once I followed one into a hole at the top of an ash stump, he ran up the trunk like a squirrel. He found himself cornered and made dashes at my hand spitting like a cat. Finally he dashed over my shoulder & fell into the hedge below and got off." EAW

The British Mammals: 1905-1910

Roe Deer

Roe. ♀

Glendoe. Apr. 2. 07.

Balgowan
15. XI.95.

Red Deer

Fallow Deer

The British Mammals: 1905-1910

[11th June from Cheltenham to town by the 5.30am train] "... and I wrote my Grouse plumage paper the whole three hours' journey, but could not get it finished; then for an hour with Barrett-Hamilton who had come over from Ireland to square up the British Mammal Book with me." EAW

Red Deer Stag

The British Birds: 1905-1910

Ted had been elected a member of the British Ornithologists Union in 1900 and although he was far too over-worked to attend many meetings he was reputedly one of its most popular members. He enjoyed the excursions to places of ornithological interest, such as Lord Rothschild's collection at Tring, and it brought him into contact with the leading ornithologists of the day. Dr. Sclater introduced him to Professor Pyecraft the famous bird osteologist with whom he subsequently enjoyed working; Ogilvie-Grant introduced him to Lord Lovat which brought him work with the Grouse Disease Inquiry; and Ted was also introduced to Eagle Clarke. Not long afterwards, Ted publicly debated the subject of penguins with Eagle Clarke and the Hon. Walter Rothschild at one of the meetings of the Union. It wasn't long before Eagle Clarke asked Ted to illustrate his revised edition of Yarrell's, *A History of British Birds*. Eagle Clarke was a noted ornithologist and the combination of his editing and Ted's illustrations promised a classic work. Ted was utterly delighted. Nevertheless, he went out of his way to point out that he had already undertaken several commitments and wondered whether it might not be better to find someone else? Eagle Clarke was adamant, however. As the publishers later noted, "it was he who was so anxious for the work to be given to Dr. Wilson." Of all of Ted's projects, in many ways this was the one that he most desired to fulfil.

As with the mammals, Ted wanted every illustration, wherever possible, to be based on personal observation of the live bird. However, the quality of optics was still not very high in the early part of the 20th Century and so the live sketches still needed to be filled in with plumage studies of dead specimens. Ted was soon occupied in making sketches and notes on the natural pose and flight patterns of birds whenever the opportunity arose, whether in the field or at the London Zoo. He also studied bird skins in Museum collections. He then combined these preparatory studies into plates designed to meet client expectations. The production of illustrations for 350 species of bird was daunting but Ted worked through them, one at a time. The quiet self-discipline of his Christian asceticism enabled him to accomplish an extraordinary amount of work. Almost every moment that he was not at work on the grouse, he was busy with his pencils and brush working on the British birds and mammals.

Ted thought that one of the more delightful aspects of the bird and mammal projects was to bring him into touch with the commissioning publishers, Oliver and Boyd in Edinburgh. He thought the two partners charmingly old fashioned, "of the Dickens type", and they got on very well. They assured Ted that the work that he was doing was taking him into "the first rank" of wildlife illustrators. One result of the connection were orders for a single plate for each of Chapman's *Bird-life of the Borders* and Nape's *Nebula to Man*, these Ted duly executed. Ted in return persuaded the Royal Society to place the publication of the *National Antarctic Expedition 1901-1904, Album of Photographs and Sketches*, which he was editing, into their hands.

In July of 1908, Ted had a meeting with Eagle Clarke and Oliver and Boyd who were full of praise for the bird work that he had so far executed. Oliver and Boyd even went so far as to give him a £50 cheque (equivalent to £3000 today) as "a reminder". This seems like quite a sum but is in line with the market rate for Ted's paintings at the time. Ted occasionally sold paintings to order, but he disliked doing so, quite apart from his other work commitments. However, it is recorded that he sold two of his pictures for around £70 (equivalent to £4000 today) during 1906. Nevertheless, it was a generous gesture from Oliver and Boyd, who knew how much work he was trying to get through. What none of them yet knew was of his intention to head South with Scott again, as these plans remained uncertain until Shackleton returned in 1909. Ted continued with the execution of bird plates and had a further meeting with Eagle Clarke and Oliver and Boyd in early 1909. Once again, they were full of praise for his work. It was almost in stark contrast to Barrett-Hamilton, who tore Ted's pictures to shreds and made him re-paint them, just as often as he praised them. However, Ted was too busy to worry and took the comments at face value.

The last Wilson family Christmas at 'Westal', Cheltenham, 1909

Shackleton returned from the Antarctic in June 1909, a hero for getting within 98 miles (176km) of the Pole, but he had failed to attain it and so had left the job for Scott to finish. Scott rapidly got his dormant plans under way and Ted was publicly confirmed as the Chief of Scientific Staff. Ted hoped that this position would help him to get a regular billet on his return, so that he could settle down with Ory, perhaps in his long-hoped for role as a Government scientist in New Zealand. Many of Ted's friends tried to dissuade him from going South again but he was already committed. His friendship and loyalty to Scott were strong and they were determined to finish together what they had started aboard *Discovery*.

Ted was now in serious difficulties with regard to meeting all of his work commitments. He was busy painting and writing at all hours of the day. It was with some relief, therefore, that as soon as Oliver and Boyd were informed of the pending British Antarctic Expedition, they agreed to postpone the fulfilment of the contract for half of the bird plates until the Expedition's return, provided that Ted met the contract for the first half of the plates before the Expedition sailed. Their letter was accompanied by another cheque to cover his "expenses". Once these arrangements were confirmed in September, Ted was naturally delighted and somewhat relieved.

It was a considerable shock to Ted, therefore, to open a letter six weeks later from Eagle Clarke. Its exact contents are unknown but Ted wrote to Oliver and Boyd in complete disbelief: "He seems quite recently to have made up his mind that my Bird Drawings are after all not at all what is wanted, and his further criticism seems to me most unnecessarily scathing... I remember the remarks which he made upon the very same pictures earlier in the year." Ted's letter crossed with one written by Oliver and Boyd, which arrived with Ted the following day: "We regret very much to inform you that neither Mr. Clarke or Ourselves are satisfied with the Bird Drawings... we fear that you have had too many other engagements on hand to permit of your giving the Bird Drawings the time and attention they require." Ted was stunned but accepted the termination of the contract without further payment.

There was, and remains to this day, considerable confusion about why the contract was cancelled. There is no doubt that Ted did have too many engagements on hand but arrangements had been made to accommodate this and it seems extraordinary to cancel them within weeks. It also seems extraordinary to praise paintings one day and condemn them the next. Ted's father suggested that the real reason was that they had decided that the book was to be published before Ted returned from the Antarctic, but it never appeared. James Thin recalled years later that the whole business was "a very painful one" but that the matter was in the hands of Eagle Clarke. He also suggested to George Seaver that if something had to be written: "... it could only be that owing to Dr. Clarke's health he was unable to carry out his intention of editing the book and asked us, as publishers to relieve him of his contract; the project was abandoned and Dr. Wilson's commission was cancelled." This is not, however, what was said at the time. Perhaps it was simply the product of the fact that Ted was wrestling on the forefront of wildlife painting, desperate to produce images of live birds and yet constrained by technical and aesthetic restrictions to his work. Perhaps as a result, his work was too much of a compromise. It seems peculiar, though, that nothing was said to him; he would happily have repainted the images, as he did with the mammals. In any case, when judged from our modern viewpoint, the plates that he completed seem no worse than those of his contemporaries. It seems unlikely that we will ever know the truth of the matter.

Ted had little time to lick his wounds. The Wilson family, including Ted and Ory, gathered at the family home at *Westal* in Cheltenham for what was to prove to be the last such family Christmas. Ted was busy with work for the Grouse Disease Inquiry, the British mammals and drawing up a scientific programme for the forthcoming Expedition, along with finding the scientists to fulfil it. As he sailed Southwards aboard *Terra Nova*, he cut a familiar figure on deck with his binoculars, watching birds. Amongst the belongings that Ted left behind were the preparatory drawings and plates for the British Birds project, in various stages of completion. They provide a unique insight into the way that Ted worked up his pictures and hold the long forgotten promise of a magnificent ornithological work. Some years after his death a few of the plates were used to illustrate Hesketh Prichard's *Sport in Wildest Britain*. Occasionally the images have been admired by eminent ornithologists and artists and occasionally there has been discussion of their publication. But mostly the pictures have lain more or less forgotten for 100 years.

Edward Wilson, watching birds from 'Terra Nova', 1910

The British Birds: 1905-1910

Plate sketches

The British Birds: 1905-1910

Robin   Willow Warbler

"My little bird-pictures are just visible proofs of my love for them, and attempts to praise God and bring others to love Him through His works, and that's why I love to give them all away and hate to sell them." EAW

Blackbird   Ringed Plover

House Sparrow

Sparrow.

Hen sparrow feeding fledgling
Fort Augustus 1957.

The British Birds: 1905-1910

Treecreeper

"Tree Creeper: Song - "Easy, easy, ease a bit, easily with it a bit" ... I saw two Creepers chasing one the other. They simply flew round and round the trunk in a spiral upwards as fast as one could swing a stone tied to a string round. So that really they appeared again before the last impression was gone. And this so close to the tree trunk that they seemed just not to touch it. Yet it was a well grown oak with many small twigs for them to run into." EAW

Jay

Crossbill

Long-tailed tit

The British Birds: 1905-1910

Snowy Owl

"I do love the Hawks and the Owls more than any other birds, except perhaps the migrant Warblers." EAW

Redshank

Avocet

The British Birds: 1905-1910

Wigeon

"Three hundred and fifty birds to paint is the hardest of all, much of the Mammal book still to do and the Grouse Inquiry Report to be got out before Christmas as well as the Antarctic preparations. I have undertaken to have it all done before leaving England."
EAW

The British Birds: 1905-1910

Rook

Cuckoo

The British Birds: 1905-1910

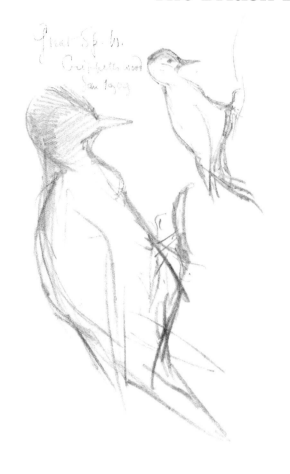

"Great Spotted Woodpecker - in Crippetts Wood and heard its cry which was shrill, rather like a Kestrel, and something like a Missel thrush. This bird was "rattling" away at the tree trunks the whole morning. Rattling is a bad word for it, the noise is absurdly like the creaking of a tall tree and also like a certain low croak that the Raven has. The noise carries a great distance and the variations in pitch from the size of the bole give it a weird character." EAW

Great-spotted Woodpecker

dropping on to
a mouse.

Flying low over
new field.   Tawny Owl. adult.
Canterbury. July 08.

Corn Bunting ♂.
Grantown on Spey
April 8.08

Bill. bluish black-grey.
Iris dark brown.
Legs oo Greyish brown.

Iris hazel brown.

Young Sandpiper.
Glencourse Pentlands
Skin is black throughout   June 27.1906.

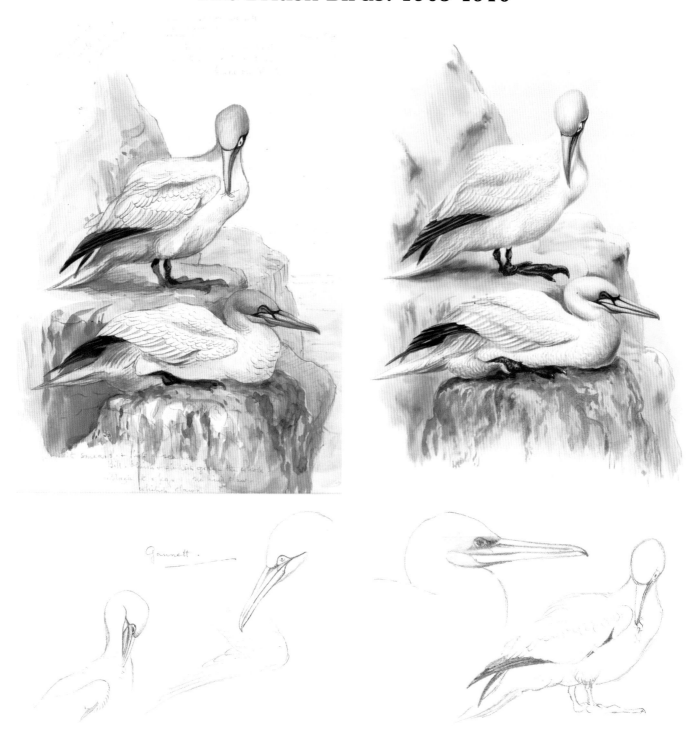

"[Messrs Oliver and Boyd of Edinburgh are] publishers of the real old stock, you would love to see them, they remind me of the Dickens type... they tell me the work I am doing (for Barrett-Hamilton and Eagle Clarke) will put me in the first rank..." EAW

Gannett

The British Birds: 1905-1910

Moorhen

Merlin

Oystercatcher

Common Chough

"We are always at work, but by no effort seem able to get ahead of it, or out of it, or even to stand still in it, - always one must go on and on to the next thing. And I do thank God that it is so, however uncomfortable it may be: rest will come when it cannot any longer be avoided, and this is not either our rest or our abiding place." EAW

Chough

House Martin

Hobby

The British Birds: 1905-1910

Little Owl

Redwing

"We, that is Eagle Clarke, W. Berry, Willie Carstairs the keeper, and self, spent the whole day on Tentsmuir and the seashore, approaching by Morton's lough. We saw things on moor, heather, rushes and sand." EAW

Kingfisher

Water Rail

Blue Tit

The British Birds: 1905-1910

Redstart

Hawfinch

Marsh Tit

Bullfinch

"I feel that every picture I draw will live and effect something after our death... I always feel so certain that I shall be given time to write and publish some of the things that are in my head, and also to paint some others, not in a hurry as I have to now, but my best possible." EAW

Paraselena. Jan. 15. 11. 9.30 pm.
Cape Evans. McMurdo Sound.

'TERRA NOVA' FINALE:
THE BRITISH ANTARCTIC EXPEDITION 1910-1912

"These days are with one for all time - they are never to be forgotten - and they are to be found nowhere else in all the world but at the Poles. The peace of God which passes all understanding reigns here in these days." EAW

The British Antarctic Expedition: 1910-1912

Amid a cacophony of hooters and cheering crowds, *Terra Nova* sailed from Cardiff on 15 June 1910, bound for the frozen South. They sailed via Madeira, South Trinidad, South Africa and Australia to New Zealand, with Ted sketching all the way. At South Trinidad, he was able to see, once again, the Trinidad Petrel that had been named for him by the ornithological authorities. From South Africa he posted home the last of his mammal and grouse work. Here, too, Captain Scott joined the ship. He had stayed behind to raise badly needed funds for the Expedition and now sent Ted on ahead to Australia to carry out fund-raising there. Fund-raising was an almost constant headache. The entire Expedition finally assembled in New Zealand from where it sailed on 29 November 1910. Despite having received a telegram from the Norwegian explorer, Roald Amundsen, informing Scott that he was "sailing South" there was still no real comprehension aboard as to what this truly meant. In fact, Amundsen had deceived everyone as to his true intentions and was deliberately setting out to forestall the British at the South Pole.

After fierce storms and a severe delay in the pack ice, the Expedition finally landed at Cape Evans in McMurdo Sound and had soon established their base. By 24 January 1911 the first major sledging party was heading South to establish supply depots towards the following season's attempt on the Pole itself. This Depot Journey was a catalogue of bad luck and human error which left the Expedition's main supply depot 30 miles further north than had been intended and with the loss of six ponies. The dogs had not performed well either. Into the middle of these concerns arrived the news that Amundsen had been found, having set up his winter quarters on the Great Ice Barrier at the Bay of Whales. This was a tremendous shock and after numerous arguments and much fretting, Scott decided to simply stick to his plans as they were laid out, rather than engaging in the race that Amundsen had apparently declared.

Edward Wilson painting at Cape Evans, 1911

Through all of these events, Ted was a bastion of calm support to Scott. Indeed, he became the confidante of almost all on the Expedition, who regarded him with considerable affection, calling him "Uncle Bill". They trusted his common-sense judgement, his personal serenity and his complete dedication to others. What they didn't know was the considerable personal effort that Ted had made, over the years, to achieve this mastery over his acid tongue and highly strung emotions, nor that the basis of this achievement lay in a strong Christian faith. He quietly organised and inspired the scientific staff to carry out an extraordinary amount of work as well as executing a great deal himself. He was forever working at his table studying biological specimens or painting up his sketches, frequently standing so as not to fall asleep. In particular, during the first months of the winter Ted executed some of his finest watercolours. It is this series of his paintings that are perhaps most widely known. The accuracy of his Antarctic work in terms of colour and detail has frequently been noted, in particular by Apsley Cherry-Garrard. He later wrote of these paintings that "If you look at a picture of a parhelion by Wilson not only can you be sure that the mock suns, circles and shafts appeared in the sky as they are shown on paper, but you can also rest assured that the number of degrees between, say, the sun and the outer ring of light were in fact such as he has represented them." It was this level of scientific accuracy, also developed with painstaking self-discipline over many years, that made Ted an important expedition artist. He was also amongst the last. On Scott's Expedition too, was the first professional photographer to head South. The work of the 'camera artist', Herbert Ponting is remarkable. Film and photograph, rather than art were, from this point on, the primary media for recording expeditions. This Expedition is the final turning point, having with it perhaps the last great expedition artist and one of the first great travel photographers, working side by side. Ted and Ponting got on famously and assisted each other with criticism and inspiration. They planned to exhibit their work together upon returning home and it seems astonishing that this was never achieved.

Berg off Cape Evans, 28 April 1911, Last day of the sun

Apart from his painting, Ted had something rather unusual planned for the winter scientific programme. The fact that they had been unable to make their base at Cape Crozier meant that a winter journey would need to be undertaken in order to secure the eggs of the Emperor Penguin at an early stage of embryonic development. It was thought that this species was a primitive form of bird and that since ontogony (the development of the individual) recapitulated phylogeny (the evolutionary development of the species) the study of the embryo would yield the scientific holy grail of the missing evolutionary link between dinosaurs and birds. The prize could not have been higher even though it now meant making a journey of considerable difficulty.

Bergs around Inaccesible Island, September 1911

Ted and his companions, Birdie Bowers and Apsley Cherry-Garrard, left Cape Evans on 27 June 1911, marching out into the winter darkness for Cape Crozier, 65 miles (120km) away. The average temperature on the journey was -60°F (-51°C); it fell as low as -77°F (-60°C). It was so cold that the pus inside their blistered frostbite froze and their teeth cracked but they persevered. At Cape Crozier they built a hut to serve as a field laboratory to study the penguins. However, shortly after they had attained the first 3 eggs they became trapped by a blizzard. Their tent blew away, shortly to be followed by the hut roof. As they lay in their sleeping bags with the blizzard raging around them, Ted passed his 39th birthday. Incredibly, when the blizzard was over, they searched and found their tent. Birdie Bowers tied himself to it whenever they stopped during the return journey, so that it didn't get away without him again. The three men arrived safely back at Cape Evans on 1 August. This was one of the most astonishing journeys to be successfully executed throughout the Heroic Age of Antarctic exploration and was immortalised in Cherry-Garrard's subsequent book, *The Worst Journey in the World*. The scientific hypotheses on which it was based subsequently turned out to be false but such striving for knowledge is part of the process of attaining Truth.

The main Polar Party left Cape Evans on 1 November 1911. Following his experience on the British National Antarctic Expedition, Scott's assault on the Pole utilised several modes of transport, tractors, dogs and ponies, with mixed degrees of success. From the bottom of the Beardmore Glacier the sledges were man-hauled, as planned. At the top of the Beardmore Glacier Scott announced the final team for the Pole, with 5 men rather than 4, amongst which Ted was delighted to be included. The team of Scott, Ted, Bowers, Oates and P.O. Evans achieved the South Pole on 17 January 1912. Here they found Norwegian flags and a tent; Amundsen had beaten them to it. It is doubtful if Ted was very bothered. He dutifully sat and sketched; they took their positions, posed for photographs and headed north again a couple of days later. It was on the way back down the Beardmore Glacier that things started to go badly wrong. Evans was becoming noticeably weak. They stopped to collect geological samples in the area around Mount Buckley, as they had been requested to do by senior geologists, and picked up 35lbs (16kgs) of specimens. Amongst these was the first known Antarctic specimen of *Glossopteris*, a critical species in the debate on the origin of the Earth's continents. Ted also made detailed geological notes and sketches as they descended the Beardmore Glacier. They were to be his last. His time was increasingly taken up nursing sick companions. Evans died at the bottom of the Beardmore Glacier; Ted thought that he had injured his brain in a series of falls. The remaining four men soldiered on but once on the Ice Barrier experienced unseasonably low temperatures. Instead of the expected temperatures around -20°F (-29°C) they experienced temperatures down to -40°F (-40°C). These altered the surface of the snow and made it almost impossible to pull their sledge. One by one they became frost-bitten, Oates so badly that he committed suicide in a bid to save his companions, walking out of the tent with the words "I am just going outside and may be some time". It was not enough. Badly frost-bitten, dehydrated and short of food and fuel, Ted, Bowers and Scott perished in their tent around 29 March, 11 miles (20km) short of their main One Ton Depot. The following Spring they were buried upon the Great Ice Barrier by a search party, which also recovered their scientific specimens, their diaries and the final sketch books of Edward Adrian Wilson.

At the Pole: L-R: Wilson, Bowers, Evans, Scott and Oates

Select Bibliography
and
Further Recommended Reading

Barrett-Hamilton G.   *A History of British Mammals*, parts 1-21. Illustrated by
& Hinton M.A.   E.A.Wilson & Guy Dollman. London, Gurney & Jackson, 1910-1921

Chapman, A.   *Bird-life of the Borders: Records of Wild Sport and Natural History on Moorland and Sea*. 2nd edition. London, Gurney & Jackson, 1907 [Frontispiece by E.A.Wilson]

Cherry-Garrard, A.   (ed.) *The South Polar Times*, Vol. III. London, Smith Elder & Co., 1914
The Worst Journey in the World. London, Constable, 1922

Fox, W.   *Terra Antarctica: Looking Into the Emptiest Continent*. San Antonio, Texas, Trinity University Press, 2005

Higgins, H.   *The Semilunar Fibro-cartilages and Transverse Ligament of the Knee Joint*, illustrated by E.A.Wilson. London, *Journal of Anatomy and Physiology* Vol. 29, 1895

King, H.G.R.   (ed.) *Edward Wilson: Diary of the 'Terra Nova' Expedition to the Antarctic 1910-1912*. London, Blandford Press, 1972
(ed.) *South Pole Odyssey: Selections from the Antarctic Diaries of Edward Wilson*. Poole, Blandford Press, 1982

Knipe, H.R.   *Nebula to Man*. London, Dent, 1905 [part illustrated by E.A. Wilson]

Lack, D.L.   *Some British Pioneers in Ornithological Research 1859-1939*. London, *Ibis*, Vol. 101 #1, 1959

Leslie A.S. &   (eds.) *The Grouse in Health and in Disease: Being the Final Report*
Shipley A.E.   *of the Committee of Inquiry on Grouse Disease*. London, Smith Elder & Co., 1911

Prichard, H.   *Sport in Wildest Britain*. "Illustrated from water-colour paintings by Dr. Edward A. Wilson". London, William Heinemann, 1921

Roberts, B.   (ed.) *Edward Wilson: Birds of the Antarctic*. London, Blandford Press, 1967

Rolleston, H.D.   *Diseases of the Liver, Gall Bladder and Bile-Ducts*. Illustrated by E.A.Wilson. Philadelphia, W. B. Saunders, 1905

Savours, A.   (ed.) *Edward Wilson: Diary of the Discovery Expedition to the Antarctic Regions 1901-1904*. London, Blandford Press, 1966

Scott, R.F.   *The Voyage of the Discovery*. London, Smith Elder & Co., 1905
Scott's Last Expedition. London, Smith Elder & Co., 1913

Seaver, G.   *Edward Wilson of the Antarctic: Naturalist and Friend*. London, John Murray, 1933
Edward Wilson Nature Lover. London, John Murray, 1937
The Faith of Edward Wilson. London, John Murray, 1948

Shackleton, E.H.   (eds.) *The South Polar Times*, Vols. I & II. London, Smith Elder &
& Bernacchi, L.C.   Co., 1907

Skelton, J.V. &   *Discovery Illustrated: Pictures from Captain Scott's First*
Wilson, D.M.   *Antarctic Expedition*. Cheltenham, Reardon Publishing, 2001

Walker, C.E.   *Old Flies in New Dresses: How to Dress dry Flies with the Wings in the Natural Position and Some New Wet Flies*. Illustrated by E.A. Wilson & the author. London, Lawrence & Bullen, 1898

Wilson D.M. & Elder D.B.	*Cheltenham in Antarctica: the Life of Edward Wilson*. Cheltenham, Reardon Publishing, 2000
Wilson E.A.	*Notes on Antarctic Seals collected during the Expedition of the 'Southern Cross'* in *Report on the Collections of Natural History made in the Antarctic Regions during the Voyage of the 'Southern Cross'*. London, British Museum (Natural History), 1901

The Birds of the Island of South Trinidad. London, *Ibis*. 8th series, Vol.4 #14, 1904
On Some Antarctic Birds. London, *Proceedings of the IVth International Ornithological Congress*, 1905
Exhibit and Discussion on Albino Penguins (with W.E.Clarke, & Lord Rothschild). London, *Bulletin of the British Ornithologist's Club*, Vol.15 #114, 1905
International Bird Protection. London, *Bird Notes and News*, No.10, July 1905
Penguins. London, *Bird Notes and News*, No.11, October 1905
The Distribution of Antarctic Seals and Birds. London, *Geographical Journal*, Vol. 25 #4, 1905
The Emperor Penguin. London, *Ibis*. 8th series, Vol.5 #18, 1905 [Summary of a lecture given at the Royal Institution on 27 January 1905. Reprinted from *The Times*, 28 January 1905]
Aves, in *National Antarctic Expedition 1901-1904, Natural History Vol. II Zoology*. London, British Museum (Natural History), 1907
Mammalia, in *National Antarctic Expedition 1901-1904, Natural History Vol. II Zoology*. London, British Museum (Natural History), 1907
National Antarctic Expedition 1901-1904: Album of Photographs and Sketches with a Portfolio of Panoramic Views. London, Royal Society, 1908
The Changes of Plumage in the Red Grouse (Lagopus scoticus) in Health and in Disease. London, *Proceedings of the Zoological Society of London*, December 1910 [n.b. the ZSL proceedings for 1909/1910 contain articles by Shipley, Fantham and others involved with the Grouse Disease Inquiry which are illustrated by E.A.Wilson]
The British Antarctic Expedition. London, *Geographical Journal*, Vol 39 #6, 1912

Exhibition	*"Discovery" Antarctic Exhibition, Bruton Galleries Illustrated Catalogue*. London, The Bruton Galleries, 1904
Exhibition	*British Antarctic Expedition 1910-1913. Exhibition of Antarctic Sketches and Water Colours, Drawings of Swiss and Norwegian Scenery, Sketches of Birds etc. By Dr. Edward A. Wilson at the Alpine Club*. London, Wm. Clowes & Sons, 1913

There are a large number of publications relating to Captain Scott's two Antarctic expeditions containing illustrations by E.A.Wilson and references to his life and work. These are, however, too numerous to provide a comprehensive listing.

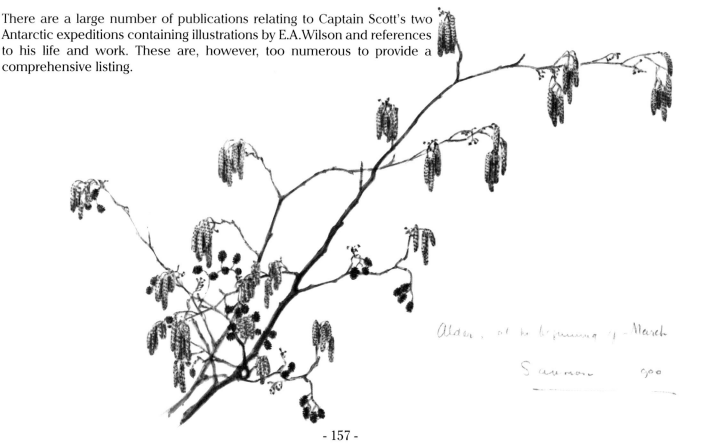

List of Illustrations and Copyright Acknowledgements

The vast majority of the images in this book are either in pencil, water-colour or a combination thereof, utilising several wash techniques. A few images are in pen and ink. Edward Wilson also occasionally used chalk and charcoal. He never, in so far as we have discovered, used oils. As pictures in ink, pencil, chalk or water-colour are quite distinctive we have seen no need to list the media of each picture.

****

With thanks to:

SPRI = Scott Polar Research Institute
NHM = Natural History Museum, London (Picture Library reference)
CAGM = Cheltenham Art Gallery and Museum
CC = Cheltenham College
CPL = Cheltenham Public Library
SGH = Saint George's Hospital Medical School
DHT = Dundee Heritage Trust
Private = Numerous Private Collections

****

Endpaper

Kingustie, Scotland. 13 April 1908 © private

Frontispieces

p01 - Text: "Sketches, Ted Wilson". Undated © CAGM 1995.55.170
- [Late summer hedgerow]. Undated © private
p02 - Head of a Slowworm, Crippetts Wood. 12 May 1898 © private
- Lizard. April 1896 © private
- Bramble (flower) from the hedge, Briar Brake, *The Crippetts*. 27 August 1896 © private
- *Pterostenus*. Undated © private
- Ladybird, found all over the Gorse, *The Crippetts*. 23 March 1898 © private
p03 - An Ichneumon Fly, *Ryssa persuasoria*. Undated © Private
- Bramble (fruit) from the same bush as above. 27 August 1896 © private
- Goldcrest. Undated © private
- *Mus sylvaticus* [Wood Mouse] caught on bacon, Crippetts Wood. March 1898 © NHM T36136
- [Bush Cricket] Found on a Willow Leaf, *The Crippetts*. August 1896 © private
p04 - Green Woodpecker, British Birds Project. 1905-1910 © SPRI 1862
p05 - Orkney Voles, from life at Paynetts. 14 September 1905 © NHM T36182
p06 - Marsh Tit. Undated © SPRI 1926
p07 - Wild Cherry, *The Crippetts*. 12 April 1896 © private

PART ONE: 1872-1904

The Childhood Years: 1872-1891

The Student Years: Cambridge 1891-1895

Char. 2 lbs.
Horstad, Norway. July 1893.

Ted Wilson.

The Student Years: London 1895-1898

p38   - St. George's Hospital, First Boat: L-R: G.E.Orme; A.deW.Snowden; R.Abercrombie; H.H.Stiff; E.A.Wilson. 1897 © SGH

p39   - Edward Wilson. Undated [c. 1898] © CAGM 1995.550.183

p40   - [*The Crippetts* Barn, Cowsheds and Farmhouse, with Doves]. 1896 © private
       - From *The Crippetts*. April 1896 © CAGM 1995.550.170
       - *The Crippetts* Barn and Cowsheds. 1896 © CAGM 1995.550.170

p41   - [Cheltenham College Chapel, from *Westal*]. Undated © CAGM 1995.550.170
       - Pied Wagtail, *The Crippetts* Pond, Life. April 1896 © private
       - *Equiretum magnum*, Shurdington. 23 April 1896 © private
       - [Bluebell], *The Crippetts*. 23 April 1896 © private

p42   - Kite, four years old ['Milan']. 1896 © private
       - Water Violet, Epping Forest. 10 May 1896 © private
       - Kestrel, South Kensington Museum. Undated © private
       - Mullein, Henley on Thames. 23 July 1896 © private
       - Fox-tail Grass, Epping Forest. 13 May 1896 © private

p43   - Blackthorn, *The Crippetts*. August 1896 © private
       - Oak spangles. 12 August 1896 © private
       - Water Shrew, *The Crippetts*. August 1896 © NHM T36129
       - Brown Rat, *The Crippetts*. August 1896 © NHM T36157
       - *Sirex Gigas*, *The Crippetts*. 27 August 1896 © private

p44   - Wasps nest, *The Crippetts*. 29 August 1896 © private
       - Musk Beetle, Tewkesbury. 1896 © private
       - Honeysuckle, *The Crippetts*. August 1896 © private
       - Swallow roosting, *The Crippetts* Cowshed. August 1896 © private
       - [Ploughmans Spikenard], *The Crippetts*. August 1896 © private

p45   - Immature Cuckoo, shot at Crippetts Wood. August 1896 © private
       - [Thistle], *The Crippetts*. 18 August 1896 © private
       - [Unidentified yellow flower]. 28 August 1896 © private

p46   - [Caterpillar], Regent's Park. 31 August 1896 © private
       - Vociferous Sea Eagle, London Zoo. September 1896 © private
       - [Fungi], Hyde Park. 7 September 1896 © private
       - Lesser Kestrel, London Zoo. September 1896 © private
       - Small red ant, Delamere Terrace, London. 7 September 1896 © private
       - [Fungi], Hyde Park. 7 September 1896 © private

p47   - Peregrine Falcon, London Zoo. September 1896 © private
       - Barn Owl, London Zoo. September 1896 © private
       - [Unidentified insect], London. September 1896 © private
       - [Unidentified insect], London. September 1896 © private
       - Golden Plover, London Zoo. September 1896 © private
       - Ochrea, Hyde Park. September 1896 © private

p48   - Gloucester Valley from *The Crippetts*. Undated © CC 002
       - Cheltenham from *The Crippetts*. Undated © CAGM 1995.550.170
       - Leckhampton Hill from *The Crippetts*. Undated © CAGM 1995.550.170

p49   - Surface of liver with nodular hyperplasia, *Diseases of the Liver*. P^d 1905 © private
       - Liver growths, secondary to carcinoma of the rectum, *Diseases of the Liver*. P^d 1905 © private
       - Papillomatous form of carcinoma of the gall bladder, *Diseases of the Liver*. P^d 1905 © private
       - Large intrahepatic calculi, *Diseases of the Liver*. P^d 1905 © private
       - Chronic cholecystitis with calcification, *Diseases of the Liver*. P^d 1905 © private
       - Early Purple Orchid, from Dorsetshire, Battersea. 11 April 1897 © private

p50   - Hyde Park Corner [from roof of St. George's Hospital]. September 1896 © private

p51   - From Caius House, The River, Albert Hall and Colonial Institute. 3 June 1897 © CC 008
       - Knightsbridge. 1897 © SGH
       - Letter: "My Dear Little Cherub". 26 May 1897 © SPRI MS861d
       - Fallow Deer, Battersea Park. Undated © private

p52   - [Grey] Partridge, unfinished. December 1897 © private
       - Leaves collected in Crippetts Wood. December 1897 © private
       - Tawny Owl, *The Crippetts*. December 1897 © private
       - Cup Moss, *The Crippetts*. December 1897 © private
       - On dead Hazel, *The Crippetts*. December 1897 © private

Eagle Owl young. July 1893. Horstad, Norway.

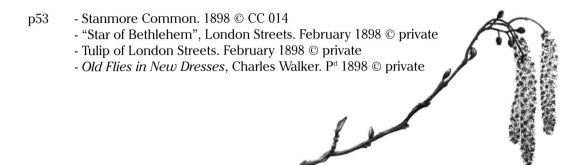

p53   - Stanmore Common. 1898 © CC 014
        - "Star of Bethlehem", London Streets. February 1898 © private
        - Tulip of London Streets. February 1898 © private
        - *Old Flies in New Dresses*, Charles Walker. P^d 1898 © private

The Tuberculous Years: 1898-1901

p54   - Edward Wilson with 'Puggie' the Red Squirrel, *The Crippetts*. April 1898 © CAGM 2004.114
p55   - Edward and Oriana Wilson on their wedding day. 16 July 1901 © CAGM 1995.550.186
p56   - Colour notes. *Westal*, Cheltenham. March 1898 © private
p57   - [Gloucester from *The Crippetts*]. Undated © CC 012
        - Snow on Bredon Hill from *The Crippetts*. Undated © CC 016
p58   - Stoat, adult female, *The Crippetts*. May 1898 © NHM T36119
        - 'Puggie' the Red Squirrel, *The Crippetts*. April 1898 © NHM T36121
        - [House] Sparrows, *The Crippetts*. May 1898 © private
        - *Oxalis*, Wood Sorrel, *The Crippetts*. April 1898 © private
        - Kestrel's egg, Crippetts Wood. March 1898 © private
p59   - [Newt Tadpole]. 21 April 1898 © private
        - [Adolescent Newt]. 21 April 1898 © private
        - [Great Crested Newt], female. 21 April 1898 © private
        - Smooth Newt. 20 April 1898 © private
        - Smaller Crested Newt. 20 April 1898 © private
        - Primrose, a single plant from Cowper's Hill. April 1898 © private
p60   - *Hårstad* [The Farm], Norway. June 1898 © CC 080
        - Pyrola [Norway]. July 1898 © private
        - Crinkleberry [Norway]. 28 July 1898 © private
        - Common Scoter, adult male, *Hårstad*, Norway. June 1898 © private
        - Saxifrage [Norway]. July 1898 © private
        - Bog Cranberry [Norway]. June 1898 © private
p61   - On Mountain tops, snow level [Norway]. June 1898 © private
        - The Mosquito Beast, *Hårstad* [Norway]. July 1898 © private
        - Bear-berry, Norway. 20 July 1898 © private
        - The Cleg beast and his head, *Hårstad* [Norway]. July 1898 © private
        - *Cassiope hypnoides* [Norway]. 11 July 1898 © private
        - A Cleg Beast, *Hårstad* [Norway]. 25 July 1898 © private
        - [Flower study, Norway]. June-July 1898 © private
p62   - Sey, Bindal River, Norway. June-July 1898 © private
        - Long-tailed Duck, adult female, *Hårstad*, Norway. June 1898 © private
        - Starved Sea Trout, Bindal River [Norway]. June 1898 © private
        - Black and White Guillemot, Sea Pool, *Hårstad* [Norway]. June 1898 © private
p63   - Alps from Zurich, Switzerland. 30 October 1898 © CC 065
        - Zurich, Switzerland. 31 October 1898 © CC 066
        - Davos, Switzerland. 1898 © CC 062
        - First Snow, Davos, Switzerland. 2 November 1898 © CC 061
p64   - Sunset studies, Tingenhorn, High Alps, Switzerland. Undated © CC 045, 046, 047, 052, 165
p65   - Seehorn Restaurant by the Lake, Davos, Switzerland. 1899 © CC 042
        - Davos [Switzerland]. 1899 © CC 060
        - Hazel Grouse, Yerper [Switzerland]. Undated © private
        - Siskin, female, Davos [Switzerland]. April 1899 © private
p66   - [Alpine scene] Davos [Switzerland]. Undated © CC 070
        - Davos, accurate colouring. [Alpine scene notes]. Undated © CC 070
        - Crocuses, Davos [Switzerland]. April 1899 © private
        - [Violas] Tifenkasten, Switzerland. 3 May 1899 © private
        - Spring Gentian, Rigi, Switzerland. March 1899 © private
p67   - Sunset, *Hårstad*, [Norway]. July 1899 © CC 081
        - Sunset, Ingelstad, Norway. July 1899 © CC 085
        - [Unlabelled Norwegian sunset]. [Undated] © CC 116
        - [Unlabelled Norwegian sunset]. [Undated] © CC 127

'Discovery' Interlude:
The British National Antarctic Expedition 1901-1904

PART TWO: 1904-1912

Ireland: 1905

The Grouse Disease Inquiry: 1905-1910

p99 - Male Grouse: white-spotted, red type, *The Grouse in Health and in Disease.* Pᵈ 1911 © private
- Female Grouse: buff-barred type, *The Grouse in Health and in Disease.* Pᵈ 1911 © private
- Male Grouse: red type, winter plumage, *The Grouse in Health and in Disease.* Pᵈ 1911 © private
- Female Grouse: summer plumage, *The Grouse in Health and in Disease.* Pᵈ 1911 © private
p100 - Feet of Red Grouse, plate XIII, *The Grouse in Health and in Disease.* Pᵈ 1911 © private
p101 - Female Grouse, feathers, plate XII, *The Grouse in Health and in Disease.* Pᵈ 1911 © private
p102 - Scottish landscape. Undated © CC 157
- Scottish landscape, unfinished. Undated © CC 158
p103 - Scottish landscape with Gulls. Undated © CC 153
- Scottish Landscape, Fort Augustus. Undated © CC 159
p104 - Ptarmigan. Undated © SPRI 1468
- Head of Ptarmigan, *The Grouse in Health and in Disease.* Pᵈ 1911 © private
- Ptarmigan sketches. Undated © private
p105 - Black Grouse displaying (watercolour). Undated © SPRI 1841
- Head of Blackcock, *The Grouse in Health and in Disease.* Pᵈ 1911 © private
- Black Grouse displaying (pencil). Undated © private
- Black Grouse sketches. Undated © private
p106 - Loch Ness at Fort Augustus. Undated © CC 160
p107 - [Hare]. Undated © NHM T36177
- Birch and Bracken, Fort Augustus. 1907 © private
- Bird sketches. Undated © private
p108 - Landscape, Fort Augustus. Undated © CC 156
- The Kirk at Fort Augustus. Undated © CC 154
p109 - The Monastery at Fort Augustus. Undated © CC 175
p110 - Red Grouse with young chicks, *The Grouse in Health and in Disease.* Pᵈ 1911 © private
p111 - *Ornithomyia lagopodis*, *The Grouse in Health and in Disease.* Pᵈ 1911 © private
- Grouse Intestines, various plates, *The Grouse in Health and in Disease.* Pᵈ 1911 © private
- *Leucocytozoon lovati*, *The Grouse in Health and in Disease.* Pᵈ 1911 © private

The British Mammals: 1905-1910

p112 - Edward Wilson by A.U. Soord. 1909 © SPRI 431
p113 - Edward Wilson c.1910 © CAGM 1995.550.188
p114 - Red Squirrel, plate, *A History of British Mammals.* Pᵈ 1910*ff* © NHM T36219
p115 - Preparatory work for Red Squirrel skins plate. Undated © NHM T36163; T36156; T36216
- Red Squirrel sketches. Undated © NHM T36161
p116 - Hedgehog, plate, *A History of British Mammals.* Pᵈ 1910*ff* © NHM T36196
p117 - Brown Hare, preparatory plate. Undated © NHM T36115
- Irish and Scottish Hare skins, plate, *A History of British Mammals.* Pᵈ 1910*ff* © NHM T36211
p118 - Noctule Bat, plate, *A History of British Mammals.* Pᵈ 1910*ff* © NHM T36149
p119 - Barbastelle Bat, Shrewsbury. 26 August 1905 © NHM T36107
- Serotine Bat. Undated © NHM T36142
- Natterer's Bat, Bradfield nr Reading. 5 July 1906 © NHM T36152
- [Whiskered Bat]. Undated © NHM T36233
p120 - Head of Noctule Bat. 7 September 1905 © NHM T36141
- Long-eared Bat. Undated © NHM T36150
- Pipistrelle Bat, Copthorne, Sussex. 9 October 1905 © NHM T36204
- *Rhinolophus hipposiderus* [Lesser Horseshoe Bat]. December 1905 © NHM T36205
- Whiskered Bat, asleep. 25 November 1905 © NHM T36230
p121 - Pipistrelle Bat, plate, *A History of British Mammals.* Pᵈ 1910*ff* © NHM T36189
p122 - Killer Whale sketch. January-February 1902 © NHM T36183
- Killer Whale, preparatory plate. Undated © NHM T36184
- Killer Whale, proposed plate. Undated © NHM T36213
p123 - Harbour Porpoise, proposed plate. Undated © NHM T36193
- Common Seal, proposed plate. Undated © NHM T36217
p124 - Dormouse notes. Undated © NHM T36114
- Harvest Mouse, sketches. Undated © NHM T36158
- Bank Vole, feet. Undated © NHM T36171
- British rodent skins, proposed plate. Undated © NHM T36212
p125 - Water Shrew, plate, *A History of British Mammals.* Pᵈ 1910*ff* © NHM T36214
- Pygmy Shrew, preparatory plate with flowers. Undated © NHM T36148
- Pygmy Shrew, plate, *A History of British Mammals.* Pᵈ 1910*ff* © NHM T36220

The British Birds: 1905-1910

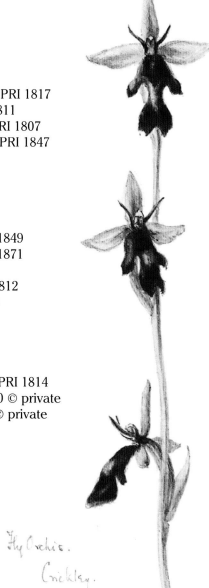

Fly Orchis.

Crickley.

'Terra Nova' Finale:
The British Antarctic Expedition 1910-1912

End-pages

Endpaper

Cover

Wood Pigeon